AROUND HEATHFIELD IN OLD PHOTOGRAPHS

A SECOND SELECTION

With best wishes

23 December 1991

CHICKEN FATTING was perhaps the most important cottage industry in the whole of the Heathfield area for over a hundred years. Here a bird is being force-fed on a mobile chicken-cramming machine developed by local ironmonger Harry Neve of Station Road. A measured amount of food is forced into the bird's crop by pressing the foot treadle. Note the raised chicken coops (protection against rats and a more convenient height to handle the poultry), the ped (a crate for transporting fowl), and the bucket to carry the cram (the food mixture of oats, animal fat and milk).

A VARIETY OF TRUCKS, LORRIES AND TRAILERS – including a 30-cwt Crossley, a 3-ton Thorneycroft, a Hallford and two 1-ton Model-Ts – collect peds (crates of dead chickens) for delivery to London's Smithfield Market. The local farmers in their carts and trucks delivered their peds to collection points such as the railway station or the Crown Hotel (where produce from the neighbouring market and livestock auction could also be collected by carriers such as Routh & Stevens or Sturdy of Punnett's Town who charged 1d. per bird for carriage to London). Empty peds were returned the following day. Farmers could also leave a pole with a white flag on it at their farm entrance to signal a collection of peds was required. (*c*. 1925)

AROUND HEATHFIELD IN OLD PHOTOGRAPHS

A SECOND SELECTION

COLLECTED BY
ALAN GILLET AND
BARRY K. RUSSELL

ALAN SUTTON

Alan Sutton Publishing Limited
Phoenix Mill · Far Thrupp · Stroud · Gloucestershire

First published 1991

British Library Cataloguing in Publication Data

Around Heathfield in old photographs.
I. Gillet, Alan, *1949–*
942.251

ISBN 0-86299-950-2

Typeset in 9/10 Korinna.
Typesetting and origination by
Alan Sutton Publishing Limited.
Printed in Great Britain by
The Bath Press, Avon.

CONTENTS

INTRODUCTION

This volume is a companion to *Around Heathfield in Old Photographs* which was published in November 1990. The undoubted success of the first volume – its initial print run was sold out within months of publication – has allowed us the luxury of presenting another 290 photographs of Heathfield and its surrounding villages for general appreciation. Moreover, this selection has given us the opportunity to look in some detail at the photographic history of Mayfield during the last century, thus redressing its omission (due to pressure of space) from the first selection.

Around Heathfield in Old Photographs: A Second Selection incorporates old photographs which have been brought to our attention since the last book was published. Indeed, it is a matter of great pride to us both that so many original photographs have materialized from attics and drawers as a direct result of the local interest awakened by the first book. Also, further information about photographs in the first book has been supplied, naming individuals in illustrations or suggesting exact locations. Among the information we have received is the following. Cover: the man in the monkey disguise is Charlie Ryder (later to run his own garage and Heathfield's cinema); p. 24: the driver of the hackney carriage is Joseph Cornford; p. 47: the entrance to the Half Moon Inn appears behind the soldier collecting for The Heathfield Tobacco Fund; p. 49: the ARP Warden is Frank Neve; p. 97: should read Stream Cottages; p. 108: the invalid in the spinal carriage is David Woodgate; p. 111: standing next to the faggot stack is Mr Porter; p. 115: Frary Walk (not Friary) takes its name from the two children of the land-owner, *Fr*eda and *Mary* Sinden; p. 143: the three aged gamekeepers are Sam Oliver, Ned Vine and Nipper Durrant.

We hope that you enjoy this second opportunity to saunter along the local byways of this particularly lovely area of East Sussex.

SECTION ONE

Heathfield

AN AMAZING PHOTOGRAPH OF A TEAM OF SIX OXEN, drawing a Sussex wagon laden with coal, turning left from Station Road into the High Street. Apparently, this was a weekly visit from Possingworth to collect coal from the goods yard at the railway station. The building behind is Barclays Bank (built for Lewes Old Bank) before it had its extension of a second gable added on the left in *c.* 1912. (*c.* 1907)

LOOKING EAST FROM TILSMORE CORNER along what is now the High Street. At the time of this 1905 postcard, the north side of the road is partly developed (from 1897 onwards); Mutton Hall Hill is still heavily wooded; and there is no building at all on the south side, in what was still open farmland, between the long demolished inn, the Welcome Stranger (landlord Thomas Blackman), seen on the right, and the Union Church (built 1900–1).

HEATHFIELD & WALDRON FIRE BRIGADE was formed in 1924, with Charlie Ryder (note his garage behind) as the Chief Officer. The brigade were all volunteers and were initially called out by maroons, although later an electric belt-driven siren was installed. The first men to arrive at the station on Tilsmore Road would drive off in the fire engine (this one supplied by the Stanley Fire Engine Company), while the latecomers had to get to the scene of the fire in any way they could. Charlie Ryder was also responsible for building the cinema, The Picture House, on the left, with the Masonic Lodge above. (*c.* 1925)

HEATHFIELD'S FIRE STATION was intially on the opposite side of Tilsmore Road where Southdown Bus Depot stood and where Southern Boat Centre now stands. It was then a one-storey building, constructed largely of asbestos. The bus company later raised the roof to allow double-decker buses to operate from here. During the war years the brigade was taken over by the National Fire Service. Among those included here are: Fred Pilbeam, Tom Appleby, Jack Neve, Reg Ford, 'Skipper' Ernie Phillips, Peter Bean, Fred Mansfield, Ken Angood, Frank Feist, Bob Bean, Ernie Phillips.

HEATHFIELD'S SECOND AMBULANCE was an American Packard, with a disinctive white cross on a red background painted on its side. The ambulance service was also undertaken by the firemen, with both vehicles being driven to fires etc. There was also a scheme where families could buy an 'Ambulance Ticket' which then allowed the family free transportation to hospital – other members of the public had to pay for each journey! Initially the ambulance shared the Fire Station garage, but later it had to be garaged at Caffyns next door (and later still at Heathfield Hotel). (late '30s)

A HANDCART advertising the business of A.F. Smith, Hot Water Fitter and Sanitary Engineer. Originally a Builders Merchant in Hailsham, he opened his second branch on the site of what is now Heathfield Ironmongers. The wooden workshop is still there, set behind the High Street shop, and is now used as a storeroom. Raised: Ernie (Pop) Phillips, H. Haffenden, -?-, Stan White. Standing: -?-, Charlie Reeves (worked as a farrier in the smithy at the rear), -?-, -?-, -?-, -?-, Dave Reeves (became blacksmith at Five Ashes). Seated: T. Axell, Charlie Lade (Manager). (*c.* 1910)

HEATHFIELD IRONMONGERS moved into A.F. Smith's High Street site in *c.* 1920. As well as being a general ironmongers, the firm's early advertising mentions that it was an agent for agricultural implements and was also a plumbing engineer for both water and gas installations. Because there was no pavement at the roadside, a passing lorry once tore off the corrugated metal canopy above the original shop frontage. Posed between the galvanized buckets, bins and scuttles are Charlie Lade (front shop manager), Bert Neve, -?-, Cecil Barrow, -?-, George Axell, Alf Rogers, Ernie Phillips (originally workshop manager and later overall manager). (*c.* 1925)

A CHARABANC is crank-started outside C.B. Ryder's garage on the north side of the High Street, where Heffle Estates now stands. C.B. Ryder established his business on this site at the end of the First World War, in conjunction with J.B. Hook. They specialized in both mechanical and electrical engineering. In 1923 C.B. Ryder's new garage premises were built directly opposite (bought in 1937 by Caffyns Ltd). He also had Heathfield's first purpose-built cinema, The Picture House, constructed alongside, together with the Masonic Hall above. (*c.* 1920)

LOOKING EAST ALONG THE HIGH STREET, with the adjoining shops of the Atkinsons on the right. Miss Maude Atkinson specialized in women's clothing while Albert ran a hardware store which also sold china and glass items. The shed on the forecourt of the balconied premises of Erreys has a striped barber's pole outside, advertising George Hickmore's hairdressing business.

LOOKING WEST ALONG THE HIGH STREET towards the wooded hill at Tilsmore Corner. The Union church was constructed in 1900–1. The original three-storeyed central section to Caffyns Garage was built in 1912, with a car showroom added on the left soon after. The pace of life seems to have been so much slower without motorized transport on the roads.

THE CORNER OF CHURWELL ROAD (the original spelling) was dominated by a large clothing and shoe shop, run initially by Long & Co., with its entrance on the corner itself. Later a new partnership was formed to run the business: Long, Fry & Howes.

THE ORIGINAL PARADE OF SHOPS on the south side of the High Street, built in 1910 by Mr Rich – who also built a stable and workshop down the twitten. It shows the business premises of: A Hart (greengrocer); R.G. Lee (paint and decorating materials) – originally a dairy; Baxters of Lewes (postcard publisher and stationery), later run by the Misses Nias; Oliver Atkinson (bicycles); William Toye (hardware). He delivered throughout the area in a gypsy style caravan and took the shop's name from the Lighthouse brand of paraffin he stocked.

THE WARTIME WORKSHOP OF STRANGE ELECTRICAL. During 1941 Len Strange transformed his radio and electrical workshop to produce essential aircraft parts – and occasionally magnificent 'souvenirs' crafted from the wreckage of locally crashed Luftwaffe aircraft (items which were then sold for the local 'Spitfire Fund'). Apart from Len (centre) – who served as a Special Constable at night – the average age of his mechanics was fifteen and a half. (*c.* 1944)

TICEHURST'S SINGER DELIVERY VAN has just received a fresh coat of paint and new sign-writing from Streatfield's carriage works on Streatfield Road. C.W.A. Ticehurst established his business in 1930 in what is now the adjoining sports shop. He originally specialized in music, selling pianos, records and wind-up gramophones. In 1936–7 the shop was used by EMI for the experimental reception of television signals. The business moved to its current premises in *c.* 1958. (*c.* 1937)

EDWARD ERREY BEGAN HIS BUSINESS dealing in second-hand furniture at Punnetts Town in *c.* 1900 and soon moved to a prime site on Heathfield High Street where he dealt in new furniture and carpets. In 1910 he expanded his business to include a printing works which was set up in the left side of the shop. The whole shop was gutted by fire in 1972.

EDWARD WATSON established his business in 1873 when, as a farmer at Dallington, he began valuing farm stock and later conducting auctions at Hailsham. He went into partnership with his son and brother-in-law in *c.* 1897 and had the single-storey office accommodation known as The Willows built on Mutton Hall Hill in 1905. (*c.* 1908)

E. WATSON & SONS' BUSINESS as auctioneer, estate agent and surveyor had so expanded that larger office premises were urgently required. Here we see the distinctive building on the corner of Station Road under construction in 1910.

LOOKING UP MUTTON HALL HILL before the development of the left side where the Roman Catholic church now stands. Many of the properties were originally shops. For instance, in the 1920s businesses operating on the south side of Mutton Hall Hill included: Britannia Mill; George Sands' cycle shop; a tailor's; a dairy; a cobbler's; Heathfield & Waldron Gas Co.'s showrooms; a cake shop; William Vine's butcher's shop at the Tower Street junction, which gave its name to Vine's Corner. A lane on the right led down to Paine's garage and Carlswood Hill.

THE CAR REPAIR WORKSHOP OF JAMES A. PAINE was sited down a lane halfway up Mutton Hall Hill, with two petrol pumps set at the lane entrance with swing arms which took the pipes high over the pavement to allow pedestrians to walk underneath. He had a block of six wooden sheds and workshops built by William Sands of Punnett's Town for only £100 in *c.* 1930. In front of the Model A Ford are Alf Parris, Eric Bean, Henry Cornford, Eric Eastwood and in the front, an apprentice, Joseph Cornford and Frank Feist. (*c.* 1930)

THE VIEW FROM THE STATION HOTEL in 1910 looks across open land towards the 55-ft high Gibraltar Tower, partly masked by trees on the skyline, which was built on the west side of Heathfield Park to commemorate the gallant defence of Gibraltar by Lt.-Gen. George Augustus Elliott, subsequently Lord Heathfield. The buildings in the centre stand on the bend of what is now Marshlands Lane, formerly Gasworks Lane because Heathfield's gasworks used to be sited here.

AN UNUSUAL VIEW FROM TOWER STREET looking down the back gardens of the properties on the south side of Mutton Hall Hill in c. 1920, showing clearly the heavily wooded nature of the area and also the lane leading off the main road where James Paine ran his garage and where Carlswood Mill operated.

MAGNIFICENT VIEWS ACROSS THE ROTHER VALLEY towards Mayfield are shown in this postcard view taken from Heathfield Golf Club. The club house was situated a short distance along Marklye Lane, on the left-hand side, with the nine hole course spanning both sides of the lane. Plans to extend to eighteen holes by taking the course across Newick Lane were proposed in 1930 but never implemented.

CHILDREN ON THE PARK RECREATION GROUND, with a much changed panoramic view behind. On the left can be seen the rail-station and the State Hall while to the right are the houses on the still wooded Mutton Hall Hill. Close scrutiny of the wooded valley of Waldron Gill, which bisects the photograph, will reveal one of the Natural Gas borehole towers to the left and a wind operated water pump directly in front of the haymakers. Most of the land on view is now extensively developed.

THE IMPORTANCE OF MARKET DAY in a rural community is evident by the number of cars parked outside the Crown Hotel and all along the neighbouring roads in *c.* 1930. Heathfield was granted its right to hold a market in 1315.

A CROWD OF INTERESTED SPECTATORS has collected on the forecourt of Bertie Breeze's Crown Hotel to watch the riders and hounds assemble. In the background can be seen the buildings and workshops of the Baltic Saw Mills Co. which opened its Heathfield branch on this site in 1931. The Crown Inn moved to its current site in the early nineteenth century where it was used as the venue for the Corn Exchange. The façade of the Inn was reconstructed in the 1920s. (*c.* 1935)

LOOKING DOWN STATION ROAD, soldiers with their swagger sticks can be seen in the distance outside Neve Bros.' hardware store, while directly behind them can be seen the four cottages built as accommodation for railway workers in *c.* 1899. (*c.* 1918)

WHAT AN AMAZING DISPLAY of stock is on show at Neve Bros.' ironmongery on Station Road. I certainly would not like to be the shop assistant responsible for bringing in all the items from the pavement at the end of the day. Harry and Fred Neve set up their shop in 1895 after trading as millwrights with their father Stephen at Punnett's Town. It was Harry who invented the chicken cramming machine while Fred established his own millwright's business on the High Street after their partnership broke up in 1912. (1925)

NATURAL GAS was accidentally discovered in Heathfield when drilling for water in the stable yard of the newly built Station Hotel in 1895. When it was also discovered only months later near the rail tunnel entrance, a company, the Natural Gas Fields of England Ltd, was set up to exploit the find (encouraged by Uckfield solicitor Charles Dawson of Piltdown Man notoriety). One of several local boreholes was drilled on the wasteland at the rear of the original Temperance Hotel.

AN ADVERTISING POSTCARD produced for the Station Hotel, postally used in 1910. The Hotel was built in *c.* 1895 and seems to have been the first building to appear on Station Road. Its first licensee was Henry Cole but by 1910 its landlord was Frederick W. Reed, who also ran an early form of horse-drawn taxi service from the stable building on the left, since flies and carriages could be hired from here. The hotel was finally demolished in 1983 for Budgens to build their supermarket.

THE STAFF OF HEATHFIELD STATION in 1918 pose on the platform with the covered walkway on the left. The station-master at the time was William A. Bridger, wearing a bow tie. The men wearing the numbered cap badges and waistcoats are the station's porters; the fact that there are six of them indicates how busy Heathfield station was in its heyday.

HEATHFIELD STATION used to be a hive of activity, especially in its goods yard. Here we see the individualized coal trucks of George Giles making a delivery at the coal yard. Note the horse-drawn coal wagon on the far left. George Giles was a local entrepeneur who was at various times also landlord of the Prince of Wales and a local hop farmer. In the background stands a container, possibly for natural gas.

WHILE DRILLING FOR A WATER SUPPLY near the mouth of the 266-yd tunnel at Heathfield station in August 1896, a strong smell of gas was noticed. On lighting a match, a flame shot sixteen feet into the air. This was only extinguished with great difficulty – by throwing wet cloths over the bore-tube. A cast-iron cap and stop-cock was later screwed on and, by 1898, gas from this bore-hole was used to light Heathfield station.

THE VIEW FROM THE MOUTH OF THE TUNNEL, looking towards the road bridge. Beyond the large water tower (needed in an age of steam trains) are two gasholders which would expand upwards as they were filled with natural gas from the nearby bore-hole. A man appears to be working at the bore-hole pipe while compressed gas cylinders can be seen lying on the ground to his left. The cylinders were filled with natural gas and sent off for laboratory testing on mine safety etc.

POULTRY FARMING was a very important local industry throughout the area, with many farms and small-holdings rearing and force-feeding poultry. Initially farmers operated independently of each other and had to organize their own marketing and transportation, whether by road or rail. Eventually, by about 1930, a co-operative was formed, calling itself the Heathfield Poultry-Keepers' Association, with G.H. Coates as the secretary. It had a membership of 500, an annual turnover of £40,000 and, in 1939, it had its own poultry packing station opened by the Minister of Agriculture. In the illustration locally produced eggs are graded and sorted, prior to being packed for national distribution. Up to four million eggs a year were marketed in this way. (1932)

SACKS OF GRAIN AND ANIMAL FOODSTUFFS are unloaded at the Poultry-Keepers' Association's own wharf in the goods yard at the railway station.

LOCAL PRODUCE DISTRIBUTION. From their own warehouse, where the unloaded grain could be processed and mixed, it was then distributed to the various members of the Association throughout the neighbourhood. Very local deliveries would probably only require the horse and cart. The truck's pneumatic tyres presumably were much more sensible when eggs were being transported. (1932)

THE TEMPERANCE HOTEL, a teetotal family hotel, originally built in 1900 across the road from the railway station. In 1924 it was rebuilt on the west side of the rail bridge by Mrs Mary Avard, while her tea room functioned as the station buffet. The single-storey garage to the left contained Heathfield's first petrol pump (imported from the USA) and was also the base for her son, Bill Avard's, taxi service.

A PANORAMIC VIEW from the top of Tilsmore Road towards Sandy Cross in c. 1910. The view takes in the rear of houses on Ghyll Road and a nursery on Leeves Common, an area now covered in the housing developments of Waldron Thorns and Leeves Way. The photograph is bisected by the Cuckoo Line, with the Ghyll Road rail bridge in the centre.

HEATHFIELD LAUNDRY. A correspondence card sent from Fred Orchard, the proprietor, to Mrs R.E. Hassell of Tanners Manor, informing her that her curtains are ready for collection, in May 1909. The laundry stood alongside Stream Bridge, at the bottom of the Waldron Gill valley, on Ghyll Road.

ALEXANDRA ROAD, as viewed from ouside the Welcome Mission Hall. The house on the left is Vale View, while the next pair of dwellings, Dorrie Lodge and Brightling House, were only recently constructed in 1911. (*c*. 1914)

HARLEY LANE, one of the lesser known roads in Heathfield, led off west from Hailsham Road until it came longside the Cuckoo Line, clearly visible on the left of this 1916 postcard. This ornate terrace of houses was built parallel to the railway and now overlooks the Cuckoo Walk.

LOOKING NORTH along the parade of shops at Hailsham Road in the snow of c. 1908. The shop with the children outside was the local newsagent and stationers, operated by R. & E. Pattenden. Next along was David Bishop's shoe shop. Further along, on the Station Road junction, is the Prince of Wales.

THE SHOP OF PHOTOGRAPHER A.D. HELLIER & CO. stood on Hailsham Road (now an auto-parts shop). A.D. Hellier was a fine professional photographer who was responsible for taking many of the best and most animated postcard scenes of Heathfield.

LOOKING SOUTH ALONG HAILSHAM ROAD, with the parade of shops beyond Lansdowne Villas on the right. (*c.* 1920)

A LADY WHEELS HER PRAM along an unmade country lane, in reality Hailsham Road. The cottage with the magnificent topiary outside is Yew Tree Cottage near Sandy Cross. (1914)

SANDY CROSS is correctly the name given to the old junction of Hailsham Road with Ghyll Road (on the left and alongside the Relfs' Sandy Cross Stores) and Sandy Cross Lane (leading off on the right to Old Heathfield). The rise on which the photographer is standing used to be the site of Sandy Cross windmill, a post-mill demolished in 1916.

SANDY CROSS LANE with the thatched Monkhurst Farmhouse on the left. The oast-house has recently had its roof and cowl replaced as part of a conversion to a private dwelling. On the brow of the hill, on Hailsham Road, is Sandy Cross windmill, a post-mill which was demolished in 1916. (1910)

THE OLD AND THE NEW BUILDINGS of the Runt in Tun. The cottage with the steps was the original Runt in Tun alehouse but landlord Tom Wheatley had the new pub built alongside in 1910 by local builder and carpenter John Curtis. It was more than ten years later, however, before the pub was allowed to sell anything stronger than beer.

A MUSIC FESTIVAL IN THE GROUNDS OF THE TAVISTOCK HOTEL which stood on raised ground to the north of the High Street to the west of Firwood Rise. A group of rather worried looking fairies and elves from Old Heathfield School pose in front of what I assume to be Heathfield Ladies Choir, who rehearsed in the Lecture Hall of the Union Church, with a massive Union Jack behind. (*c*. 1906)

HEATHFIELD SILVER BAND started life as a Fife and Drum band in *c.* 1888. Because of a donation from the poultry dealers of Leadenhall Market, it was known for several years as the 'Chicken Fatters Band'. At the turn of the century it became a military brass band, as part of the Heathfield Detachment of the Second Sussex Royal Garrison Artillery Volunteers, wore military uniforms and did its drill and practices at the Drill Hall. This is believed to be the earliest known photograph of the band and shows them marching at East Hoathly Hospital Parade in *c.* 1900.

HEATHFIELD PARK CRICKET CLUB, with their club ground within the idyllic setting of Heathfield Park, can claim a recorded history back to May 1878 when a match was played against Hadlow Down – although some cricket had been played elsewhere within Heathfield Park in the early 1800s. Many eminent local names are immediately recognizable from this team photograph of 1893. Back row: the Scorer, Edward Watson, Frederick Parris, George Knight, James Bean. Middle row: -?-, Charles Collins, George Bean, John Bourner, William Bery, William Knight. Front row: George Ticehurst, Bertram Watson.

SECTION TWO

Broad Oak

A BUSINESS CARD FOR ISAAC MOCKFORD's thriving and expanding business. His original building incorporated the two display windows to the right, with a single-storey ridge roof above each. The expansion of the post office business – he was the 'sorting office' for the whole neighbourhood – caused him to extend his premises upwards and to the left, blocking the carriage entrance which was originally alongside. The whole of the building was demolished for the road to be widened. (*c.* 1895)

LOOKING WEST along the main Burwash Road at the Halley Road/Chapel Hill crossroads. Isaac Mockford's two-storey general store and post office stands on the right while William Malpass's smithy and workshop, its position since moved, stands behind the finger-post on the left. (1911)

VENESS & BARROW opened a small grocery and provisions shop in the corner section of what had been Isaac Mockford's store. In the white weatherboarded cottage opposite, George Frost ran his business as a baker and coal merchant – a strange combination.

A SUCCESSFUL DAY'S RABBIT SHOOTING at Broad Oak is about to be celebrated with a few flagons of beer. Isaac Mockford's earlier postcards were usually signed on the front in this way; his post-1910 postcards usually had the caption (and sometimes his name) in block type. (1905)

FANCY DRESS PROCESSION as part of Broad Oak celebrations for George VI's Coronation in May 1937. The procession, led by Mrs Dorothy Mockford, is passing a bunting-clad Broad Oak House, just along from the crossroads.

THE VIEW UP SCOTSFORD ROAD with Broad Oak Elementary School on the right. It was built as a mixed elementary school in 1911 with a maximum capacity of 160 pupils aged from five to fourteen. The School House on its left was built at the same time as the headmaster's residence and now serves mainly as the school office.

A GROUP OF BOYS AT BROAD OAK SCHOOL pose with their gardening tools prior to one of their lessons on the school allotment. The tall boy in the centre, standing to attention with a fork at his shoulder, is Don Godley who, for many years, managed the local general store.

LOOKING EAST along the main road at Broad Oak, showing how the north side, with its villa residences, was developed for housing before building was started on the south. The village newsagent (still a shop today) stands on the left.

IDEN'S CORNER at Broad Oak, the old name for the stretch of main road near Iden's Lane (sometimes known as Iden's Way), is a reminder of the local link with the story of Jack Cade, since it was Alexander Iden, the newly appointed Sheriff of Kent, who mortally wounded Jack Cade with an arrow as he was playing bowls at Cade Street in 1450. The garage on the left is the early forerunner of Broad Oak Garage. (*c.* 1930)

THE LONDON TO CALAIS AIR RACE (part of the Circuit of Europe) included a stretch from Dover to Hendon via Shoreham, which took aviators across Heathfield on 3 July 1911. The French pilot Barra, with hands in pockets, was forced to land his biplane in a hayfield near Rock Hill, from where he had to telegraph for mechanics to carry out repairs. He was down for ten hours, much to the fascination of the local population, most of whom had never seen an aeroplane before and who came in their hundreds to view the sight. Although Barra finished the circuit, he was disqualified for not completing it to the satisfaction of the officials.

MECHANICS STRUGGLE to repair Barra's damaged Maurice Farman biplane, while interested onlookers watch intently.

LAYING THE WATER MAINS from the reservoir at Burwash Weald to Heathfield. The photograph is believed to have been taken somewhere in the Swiffe Lane area in c. 1920. The tie worn by Bob Elphick, third from the left, suggests he is acting as the foreman. This is presumably before he took over as landlord of the Barley Mow.

BROAD OAK CENTENARIAN, Richard 'Bodle' Holmes, was born at Pontin's Mill, the windmill at Rockhill on the Heathfield parish boundary. No specific date of birth is recorded but he claimed to have walked to church to be baptized in May 1784 'without shoes or stockings, or any covering to his head'. He worked as an agricultural labourer and died in May 1886, never having suffered from any illness. He is believed to have been 107 years old at his death and is buried at Heathfield churchyard. The photograph shows him relaxing with a clay pipe, in his traditional Sussex smock.

A BEAUTIFUL RURAL PANORAMA: a patchwork of fields and cottages stretches into the distance on both sides of Street End Lane in 1908.

BROAD OAK FOOTBALL CLUB, who played at Satinswood Farm, had a successful season in 1933–4 when they won the East Hoathly League. The proud team displaying the cup are: J. Franklin (Vice-Chairman), K. Gordon (Chairman), S. Dumbrell (Linesman), J. Pettet, R. Dumbrell (Vice-Captain), J. Davies, S. Jefferys, D. Jefferys, G. Franklin, C. Shoobridge (Trainer), F. Feist. Seated: C. Croft, L. Dumbrell (Hon. Sec.), J. Roots (Captain), F. Leeves, F. Jefferys.

SECTION THREE

Old Heathfield

THE FOCAL CENTRE OF OLD HEATHFIELD has long been the parish church and the neighbouring stone-built Star Inn. By tradition it was constructed in the late fourteenth century to house the workers and masons employed to rebuild All Saints' church which was destroyed by fire in 1380. The brick extension facing the photographer was added much later, eventually becoming a butcher's shop and more recently a private dwelling, Star Inn Cottage. (1912)

HEATHFIELD CUCKOO FAIR. Livestock auctions were an integral part of the traditional annual Cuckoo Fair, with stalls and animal dealing taking place along both Cade Street and Church Street. Here a cattle auction is in progress in *c.* 1906. The large building in the background of both this and the photograph below is the rear view of the Half Moon (now the Jack Cade).

AN OPEN-AIR LIVESTOCK AUCTION is conducted at one of the annual Cuckoo Fairs in *c.* 1920. Makeshift sheep pens have been erected on the grass alongside Church Road at the rear of the Half Moon.

CROWDS OF ADULTS, children and policemen milling around in the roadway outside the Half Moon Inn at Cade Street suggest this is a photograph taken during the annual Cuckoo Fair, which was traditionally held in the streets and fields around the pub on 14 April each year. Children are sitting on the patio wall of Henry Ticehurst's single-storey butcher's shop, with animal carcasses hanging on display. (*c.* 1905)

BARROW'S GENERAL STORE AND POST OFFICE was opened as a shop by Thomas Barrow in 1840. Until this time it had been the original Crown Inn but its licence was then transferred to the new building at the market site. The shop continued to be run by various members of the Barrow family until its closure in 1975. Heathfield's War Memorial was erected at the far end of the recreation ground. (1916)

CADE STREET with the Drill Hall on the left, its wall literally plastered with posters, stood next to the Half Moon. On the junction opposite can be seen the bakery of Alfred Allchin with its two-storey bakehouse (now converted). The photograph was obviously taken within minutes of the illustration printed below, since the lady with the bicycle has not moved. (1903)

A BROAD-WHEELED SUSSEX WAGON trundles up the main road towards Punnett's Town while a carrier's cart delivers at Streetfield Farm. Frederick Meeten was then the landlord of the Half Moon, although his wife Harriett is later listed as the licensee. He was obviously willing to send a carriage to meet customers at the railway station a mile away if requested.

LOOKING WEST along the same group of buildings on the north side of Cade Street reveals yet another shop which is now a private residence: the single-storey cottage at the entrance to Streetfield Farm, with its fine array of enamel advertisements.

A POORLY PRINTED OLD POSTCARD of Portland Square in *c.* 1905. (I dislike the way the photographer has doctored his print to give a sharper outline to the buildings and trees.) Portland Square was built in the seventeenth century of so-called Portland Stone (hence its name). The house on the right, here, Thomas Evenden's newsagent's shop, was, from *c.* 1800 until *c.* 1840, the home and workshop of Jonathan Harmer. He baked his terra cotta plaques in his own ovens, the building having previously been a bakery.

A CHARMING POSTCARD VIEW along Church Street, the road which connects Old Heathfield with Cade Street. The house on the left is Home Cottage which quite clearly used to be two cottages. Most interestingly, on the side wall which faces the road can be found three stone faces (probably the builder and his two sons) and a terra cotta head of a cooper. Because of this the property is now named Cooper's Folly. (1911)

A GROUP OF DANCERS from Old Heathfield School pose around a maypole in their smocks, aprons and bonnets. The photograph is dated August 1924.

SECTION FOUR

Punnett's Town

THREE GIRLS WALK PAST THE JUNCTION known as Chapel Cross, with arms entwined. The original Independent Chapel dated from 1787 but was soon found to be much too small and the present chapel was built in 1809. At the time George Gilbert, an ex-soldier who had fought for many years under General George Elliott before he bought Bayley (now Heathfield) Park, was the leading Independent-Congregational minister in the county, and was commonly known as the 'Sussex Apostle'. (1908)

PUNNETT'S TOWN ELEMENTARY SCHOOL was built in 1879 by local builder Samuel Piper for a total cost of £750, its meadowland site having been bought for £5 from Sampson Punnett, a direct descendant of the Frenchman, Punnette, after whom the village was named. Its initial intake was eighty-five pupils, paying weekly fees of between 2d. and 9d. (depending on parental income). The original building consisted of the large classroom and an infants room which is now used as an office. Many evacuees from London shared the school's facilities during 1940. (*c.* 1910)

THE VIEW UP SCHOOL HILL, with tall hedgerows growing on both sides rather dwarfing the small children.

HEADMASTER JAMES SMART supervises a gardening class for boys at Punnett's Town School's allotments, while the girls would have received tuition in sewing and knitting. Standing: B. Harriet, V.J. Cornford, P. Buss, D. Leeves, C. Groves, J. Venner, J. Ince. Kneeling: E. Blunden, G. Sparkes, J. Sturdy, D. Pope, A. Blunden, L. Leeves, J. Lower, J. Pettit. (*c*. 1929)

SCHOOLS IN COUNTRY COMMUNITIES often tried to encourage interest in rural activities. Here Mr E. Booth, headmaster 1940–51, wearing a protective bonnet and holding a smoke-injector, demonstrates the craft of bee-keeping in September 1946. Top row: Gladys Thompson, Ivy Pope, John Message, -?-, Ernie Ellis, David Message. Middle: Maureen Puxty, Margaret Baker, Kathleen Scott, Heather Hobden, Mr E. Booth, Stewart Barton, Edgar Jarvis, Raymond Leeves, Allan Pilbeam. Seated: Daphne Cork, Dora Message, Shirley Lower, Molly Jarvis.

REMARKABLY LITTLE HAS CHANGED since this photograph of the row of houses at the brow of the hill at Punnett's Town was taken in *c.* 1910 – except that the quality of the road surface on the left has improved and that piles of flint chippings are no longer dumped at roadsides to be used for filling potholes.

LOCAL FESTIVITIES to celebrate the Coronation of Queen Elizabeth II in 1953 included a fancy dress competition for the local children, held in the recreation ground.

A MAGNIFICENT PHOTOGRAPH of the seventy-vaned fan-tail wind-wheel above Sampson Punnett's carpentry workshop. The wheel which powered the equipment inside the workshop was dismantled in 1916, after which the building was used for storage. Christopher Cornford poses outside his general stores, which he originally rented from Sampson Punnett and then bought in 1908 for £500. The family business he established was to flourish for seventy-five years, only closing in 1983. The single-wire telegraph pole was apparently used by the post office to transmit morse code messages. (1911)

CHRISTOPHER CORNFORD'S business had expanded considerably by 1932, allowing him to extend into the buildings on either side of his original shop – and his home, behind the yew trees. On his death, his son Joe took over the shop while Jack took over the garage business which stood opposite. Interestingly, the small one-storey shed on the right was where Edward Errey began his business in *c.* 1900 – dealing originally in second-hand furniture and antiques – before moving to Heathfield. (*c.* 1950)

NORTH STREET, with James Buckman's post office and general store on the right. Standing alongside Isaac Mockford's post office delivery cart, which called daily from Broad Oak, is a young Christopher Cornford, who began his shopkeeping career with James Buckman before setting up his own shop on the main road. (1900)

WILLIAM MORRIS'S PUNNETT'S TOWN BAKERY stood on the main road, opposite the junction with North Street. At the turn of the century, there were apparently three bakers operating in the vicinity. Today the building is used by a furniture and upholstery business. (*c.* 1908)

A VIEW ACROSS THE POND at the bottom of Little Coldharbour Farm, with a night ark (for chickens) in the field. On the skyline can be seen two of the original four windmills which Punnett's Town used to be able to boast of. On the left is Blackdown Mill; it still has its cap (taken off *c.* 1935) but its sweeps have been removed. On the right is the sawmill, which was demolished in 1933. (*c.* 1930)

THE RUTTED DIRT-TRACK OF GREENWOOD'S LANE leading towards the distant windmills of Punnett's Town, is a strange choice of scene to be chosen for a picture postcard of the area. The only animation in the scene is the photographer's own bicycle on the left.

AN EARLY PHOTOGRAPH of Punnett's Town sawmill, an octagonal smock-mill which was moved from Horam in 1866 to its site on North Street. It was used as the power supply for Lower & Piper's workshop, with its three circular saws. Whenever the wind blew – even at midnight – sawing would take place. This rare example of a wind-powered sawmill ceased working in *c.* 1923 when a single fly-wheel Ruston Hornsby paraffin driven engine was installed. It was later demolished in 1933.

A ONE-TON MODEL T LORRY, used as the builders' delivery vehicle, stands outside the entrance to the sawmill on North Street. The shed ran underneath the mill while the workshop above allowed access to the stage on which Percy Leeves and Roly Lower (in apron) stand. Tree trunks are being allowed to season outside St Peter's church, prior to sawing. (*c.* 1928)

BLACKDOWN (OR 'CHERRY CLACK') MILL was moved in pieces from Biddenden to its present site in c. 1856 after the old post-mill (built in 1750) burnt down. The smock-mill was built on an octagonal brick roundel, (later widened at its base) and ceased working in 1927, when its cap and sweeps were removed. Since that time it has been renovated several times. During the Second World War it was used as an observation post with an anti-aircraft gun set up on its stump and with a searchlight in a nearby field. The photograph shows the considerable damage caused to the mill by a direct lightning strike on 27 December 1951.

THE MODEL T FORD LORRY of Dallaway Brothers, loaded up with sacks of flour. The Dallaway family have been important millers in this area for many generations and have owned Blackdown Mill since Samual Dallaway had it moved to its present site. By 1913 John Dallaway and his sons were also running Rockhill Mill near Broad Oak. The mill ceased working in 1934.

THE BARLEY MOW LANE JUNCTION, looking east along the Battle road, with Bob Elphick's inn, after the addition of its new façade and roofline, on the right. Next along stood Percy Pont's general store and post office.

SNAPPED TELEGRAPH WIRES testify to the atrocious weather conditions in March 1947, which brought down power lines throughout the neighbourhood. The buildings on the left are Percy Pont's Stores and the Barley Mow.

RIBBON DEVELOPMENT AT SPRING HILL. The row of semi-detached bungalows on the left has recently been built by George Lower and his sons George and Roly. Each house took only eight to nine weeks to construct. Blackdown Lane, to the right of 'Roedene' (built in 1934 for builder Roly Lower), leads to Blackdown Mill. Much infilling has since taken place on the right side of the road. (1935)

WELL DIGGER, JIMMY CROFT, takes a first sip of water from the 23-ft deep well he has dug through the sand rock in what would become the back garden of Homebury on Spring Hill. Before the houses at Spring Hill were built by Roly Lower, Three Cups labourer Wally Avard was employed to discover the exact position of a water supply by divining with a hazel rod, so that each house could have its own individual well. (1933)

MOTHERS POSE FOR THE PHOTOGRAPHER – there were still so few motor vehicles around in 1906 that the main Battle Road was thought to be safe enough even for this. In the white hat is Mrs Bessie Lower, with daughter Ella in the pram; in the middle of the road is Mrs Annie White.

JAMES EASTWOOD'S GENERAL STORE (and sometime sub-post office) was set back off the main Battle road at Three Cups Corner, forming a distinctive centre to the hamlet, with its pub, chapel and shop.

THE JUNCTION of the Battle and Rushlake Green roads at Three Cups Corner looks remarkably similar today, despite this postcard view being seventy years old. The white building is the rear of what was then Eastwood's general store. (1920)

CHICKEN FATTER, James Sweetman of Three Cups, at work in the back garden of the Corner House. He also farmed at Forest Farm. The cramming machine, patented by local ironmonger Harry Neve, was foot operated, allowing the cram to be forced directly into the crop of the bird while it was being held firmly by the two hands of the farmer. The bird would then be returned to its raised coop.

PUNNETT'S TOWN FOOTBALL TEAM, nicknamed The City, played on the recreation ground opposite the school. The team includes skipper Bob Elphick, then landlord of The Barley Mow, with the ball, and goalkeeper Christopher Cornford (centre, back row).

MESSAGE'S BRICKYARD at Turner's Green was one of three small brickworks in close proximity to each other, proving perhaps the undoubted suitability of the local Wealden loam for making bricks, tiles, drainpipes etc. Charles Message set up the family business in 1870 and built both Osborne House and The Laurels as family homes. The business continued until the Second World War's blackout regulations meant the open-topped kilns could not be fired. Jim Message stands on the ramp, looking down on his workmen in the clay pit: Bill Elliott, Roland Message, Eric Bean, Jim Young, Joe Cornford and Fred Catt. (c. 1925)

SECTION FIVE

Warbleton and Rushlake Green

MEMBERS OF WARBLETON FRIENDLY SOCIETY (a local insurance scheme) pose in front of the massive marquee on the Green before going inside to celebrate their annual club day (the fourth Tuesday in May) by eating a meal of roast beef followed by Christmas Pudding. The procession would march from the Green to Warbleton church for a special service and then return, accompanied by the music of the Warbleton band. The banner proclaims: 'May unity and brotherly love support our cause.'

THE NORTH END OF THE GREEN, with its range of shops, indicates how self-sufficient a small rural community like Rushlake Green's could be. The white corner shop was Booker & Osborne's general stores. To the right stood the village bakery, on the site of what used to be a mission hall, with the stables alongside sometimes used for corn storage etc. Note the stack of faggots – used to fire the oven – in the yard. Before 1900 the bakery was run by the Oxleys. Until 1921 the baker was W.B. Dumbrill; since 1921, it was long operated by the Russell family who continued to live in the property even after the business closed. (1920)

THE TELEPHONE KIOSK stood alongside the well outside George Burgess's sweet shop on the east side of the green. His post office sign hangs above the door of the single-storey extension on the left, which also served as the telephone exchange for Rushlake Green. The gabled cottages, Fern Villa, was built in *c.* 1870, probably to house the village policeman, P.C. Nathan Vincent.

CHILDREN POSE IN THE ROADWAY outside Cherry Tree Cottage, immediately north of the Horse and Groom. In 1841 this was the site of Edward Sutton's carpenter's workshop. The half-timbered Old Fern Cottages was the last building in Rushlake Green to retain its thatched roof, which was replaced by tiles in the 1930s. The motor cycle and sidecar combination appears in many postcards of this period and almost certainly is the vehicle of the photographer. (*c.* 1920)

THE SITE OF RUSHLAKE GREEN'S LAST SURVIVING SHOP: Daw's general store and post office. It was built as a grocer's shop in *c.* 1885 for Albert Atkinson – whose name can still be clearly distinguished painted on the exterior brickwork despite the fact the shop has been owned by various members of the Daw family since 1905.

THE SOUTH-EAST CORNER OF THE GREEN at Rushlake Green used to be dominated by the village school, with its distinctive bell-tower. Built in November 1873 to accommodate 140 pupils, the school continued to serve the local children until its closure in 1965. Children from the village are now bussed to Punnett's Town School for their education. Osborne House has since been built on the site of the old school. (1906)

A WHOLE GENERATION of the boys of the village pose outside the Victorian gothic facade of the village elementary school in 1906, blissfully unaware that many of them would suffer the traumas of the First World War before reaching adulthood. Among the wartime casualties from the local community would be schoolmaster, Mr Slidel.

JUST SOUTH OF THE VILLAGE GREEN and up the lane on the left, which leads to Back Lane, stood the village smithy and the wheelwright's shop (now demolished) – traditionally the village gossip shop. In 1841 Stephen Bray was both the blacksmith and wheelright, helped by his son George Bray and by Thomas Grant. By the 1871 census John and James Payne ran the two businesses. (*c.* 1920)

THE JUNCTION ALONGSIDE GREAT CROUCHES to the south of the village green. The country lane on the left of the junction is in fact the main road from Cowbeech, with Back Lane leading off to the right. The house behind the tree used to be the home of the blacksmith Stephen Bray and is now an artist's studio. (1910)

THE AUGUSTINIANS BUILT HOLY TRINITY PRIORY to the east of Rushlake Green in 1413. When religious houses were dissolved by Henry VIII in 1536 it was presented to the Attorney-General, known as Bloody Baker. Its remains, now incorporated into Priory Farm, have passed through generations of the Roberts and Darby families until its purchase in 1882 by the Roberts Dunn family. It is now the Priory Hotel.

THE WAR BILL IN TUN, with both the staff and clientele posed outside the beautiful half-tiled façade of the seventeenth-century inn. Originally called The Two Tuns, its current name is obviously an imaginative pun on the village name. The inn's rural position has meant that a hearty walk is required before a pint can be gained – unless of course a quicker and less energetic form of transport, like a bicycle or a cart, can be found.

SECTION SIX

Vine's Cross and Marle Green

LOOKING DOWN THE HILL AT VINE'S CROSS, with Dunbreck Cottages on the left. On the far right was A. Barrow's bakery and grocery shop (which also served as the village post office until c. 1908) – now a private dwelling. The small corrugated chapel, St James' church, was only built in 1911 on the site of the bakery storehouse and so does not appear. (*c.* 1908)

THE BROW OF THE HILL, looking north towards the Brewer's Arms crossroads. In the distance on the left can be seen the wooden workshop of J. Harrison. It had once been the workshop of Frederick Pinniger, local carpenter and undertaker, and used to have a saw pit inside. Directly in front can be seen the local smithy, which was only demolished in 1958 for Vine's Cross Engineers to be built. (*c*. 1940)

LOOKING UP THE HILL, then no more than an unmade country lane in appearance, with Hybank Cottages on the right. (*c*. 1910)

THE NEW GOSPEL HALL was built in Ballsocks Lane in 1911 and initially attracted an enthusiastic regular congregation. However, habits of church-going have changed considerably during this century and so, with its congregation dwindling, it was decided to close the church in the 1970s and it has since been converted into an attractive and unusual private dwelling.

THE CONGREGATION OF THE NEW GOSPEL HALL poses outside the entrance in 1912. What a fine array of headgear is on display, from flowery bonnets to flat caps; in fact, hardly any of the men and not one of the ladies is bare-headed. Beards and moustaches were obviously in vogue, too.

MARKET GARDENS AND NURSERIES have long flourished in this area of the Weald. This *c.* 1920 photograph shows a considerable range of greenhouses leading down to the valley of Waldron Gill. At this time P.E.N. Hitchins was a tomato grower at Stream Nursery on the Old Vine's Cross Road.

BRICKWORKS AT MARLE GREEN. Although the Romans built extensively in brick, e.g. the walls of their fort at Anderida (Pevensey), the art of brick manufacturing seemed to disappear in England for over a thousand years. Some magnificent buildings, such as Herstmonceux Castle in 1440, were constructed of brick but normal dwellings were still timber-framed until the eighteenth century. Small clay pits can be found throughout the area, where small brickyards would have extracted the materials required for brickmaking, all readily available throughout the Weald: clay, sand (and wood). The size of the enterprise at Marle Green, however, can still be estimated by the massive quarry alongside the site of the brickworks. (*c.* 1950)

AN EARLY PHOTOGRAPH OF THE WORKERS at the brickworks, posed outside the old continuous kiln known as the Bottom Kiln, with its giant chimney. An interesting array of tools and equipment is on view, including three different types of moulds, a 'tile and a half' mould for hand-making the larger-sized 'granny tiles' (on the left), a standard-sized tile mould (in the centre), and a brick mould (to the right). The men with trowels would have used them for sealing the kilns. To the right can be seen a 'crowding barrow' laden with fresh bricks.

THE BUILDING OF A NEW KILN in *c.* 1945. Many of the workers on view are in fact prisoners of war, mainly Italian, who were staying at The Grange but released under supervision to carry out non-military work. The corrugated drying shed behind is still to be seen, almost all that remains of the so-called 'Sussex Tileries and Brick Works Ltd'. Needless to say, none of the three great chimneys remains.

RELAXING ALONGSIDE AN EMPTY HAY CART underneath the spreading branches of a magnificent oak tree – what could be more evocative of the peace and tranquility of the English countryside? This scene was photographed at the entrance to Marle Green farmhouse in *c.* 1910.

A HORSE-DRAWN FINGER MOWER, on the right, and a horse-drawn hay rake come together for a snapshot to be taken for the farmer's family album, after the initial cutting of the hay at Tyndall's Field. In the background, but on the other side of the main road, can be seen the sixteenth-century Huggett's Farm. (*c.* 1910)

ANOTHER MOMENT OF RELAXATION for a posed photograph. The farmer sits proudly on his horse-drawn hay rake, the ladies chatter together, while the man on top of the hay wagon places his hand on his hip in exasperation, perhaps wondering why everyone else has stopped working.

ONE OF THE MORE PHYSICALLY DEMANDING ASPECTS of haymaking as the farmhands toil with their long-handled pitchforks, raising load after load of hay up to the man perched precariously on top of the almost fully-laden hay wagon. Hidden behind the hay cart is The Moorings.

HAYMAKING is at an end, the farmer and his hands pose beside the almost completed haystack.

A CHARMING SCENE AT MARLE GREEN, with Joyce Gosden as the lucky girl about to go for a drive in this small cart made much more comfortable by its car wheels and pneumatic tyres.

SECTION SEVEN

Horeham Road

A PANORAMIC VIEW OF HORAM, taken from near Scott's Pond in the open fields which were developed as the council estate in the early 1950s. This slope used to be the ideal site for tobogganning in Horam. On the left are the back gardens of properties on the High Street while the coal yard stands on the right. (*c.* 1930)

APPROACHING HORAM FROM THE SOUTH, along the main Eastbourne Road, at Brickell's Farm, with the May Garland Inn further along on the left. By the time of publication of this *c.* 1940 postcard, the road has been metalled, kerb stones have been introduced and there is even a pavement of sorts, not paved admittedly, to ensure safety for pedestrians. By this time the new spelling of Horam is universally accepted.

AN EARLY PHOTOGRAPH, certainly Victorian, of the May Garland Inn when Alfred Noakes was the licensee and landlord. What is particularly interesting is that there was then a general store and post office in the left-hand corner of the pub, also in the name of Alfred Noakes. Notice the seated gentleman in his Sussex smock or roundfrock. (*c.* 1890)

AN ADVERTISING POSTCARD for 'Ye May Garland Inn', suggesting a certain 'olde worlde' charm to the pub. By this time a magnificent gas lamp has been added to light up the forecourt but the shop and post office, which would have stood alongside the nearest car, has ceased trading. It must have been a source of amusement for the main post office to receive telegrams addressed to 'Lovely Horeham Road'. The Lovely family ran the inn for over thirty years. (*c.* 1925)

HORAM MANOR was built in *c.* 1710 on the site of an earlier building. For a while this century it became a hotel, with tea and refreshments provided at its oast-house, until it was badly damaged by fire in 1940. Today it is the site of the flourishing Merrydown Wine Company which was established in 1946.

THE MAIN JUNCTION AT HOREHAM ROAD is still heavily wooded in this c. 1920 view which pre-dates the building of the Station Hotel. It must have been hard work for anyone in the village who enjoyed an alcoholic drink at this time, with a long walk to any pub.

THE STATION HOTEL, built in 1931, was sold later that year by Hailsham Brewery to Donald Mackay for £6,000. In 1933 it was sold, again for £6,000, to Charrington's Brewery. It has changed its name several times: from its original Station Hotel, to the Horam Hotel and now it is a free house named the Horam Inn.

THE SHOPS ON THE CORNER OF THE HIGH STREET. Mrs Rosa Baker's tea house, with its delivery bicycle outside, was also a newsagents and could offer 'Accommodation for cyclists' – obviously not many cars yet. Newnham Brothers ran a family grocer's, but also sold earthenware and brushes. The next shop along was run by A.T. Waghorn the butcher, but it was soon to be taken over by the Home & Colonial. Arthur Felgate's fishmonger's shop also sold ice – a reminder that these were the days before refrigerators. (*c.* 1908)

ALONGSIDE ROSA BAKER'S TEA HOUSE was a sunken garden where refreshments were served in the summer months. (*c.* 1908)

THE BANK BUILDINGS have only recently been erected in this c. 1910 photograph. On the left is the single-storey branch of Lewes Old Bank. F.J. Tolman & Co. ran their auction and estate agency in what is now the post office. Next were the cycle specialists, Brook & Roger, with their garage workshop alongside. The next building along, apparently not yet occupied, would, for a short while, be Horeham Road post office. The final shop front was that of Frederick Turner, who combined the businesses of builder and undertaker.

TWO SOUTHDOWN LEYLAND COACHES HAVE ARRIVED, one with a removable canvas sun-roof, to collect everyone waiting outside what used to be called the Working Men's Club. There is something about the way the crowd is waiting expectantly and the fact that the woman who has left the club is wearing some sort of armband which suggests that this is not just some sort of outing waiting to set off.

THE STATION BUILDING at Horeham Road was on the 'Up' platform and, as elsewhere on the Cuckoo Line, it incorporated the station-master's residence, the main waiting room and all the offices. The building was of red brick with stone facings and originally (1880) had a mock Tudor half-timbered appearance, but this was covered in tile-hanging in 1890. Notice the milk churns on the 'Down' platform, with the small waiting shed beyond. (c. 1905)

A TRAIN STANDS ON THE 'DOWN' PLATFORM at Waldron & Horeham Road station. The number of carriages and the crowd of passengers waiting to board the train suggest it is running through to the seaside at Eastbourne. The LV notice on the end carriage presumably indicates 'Last Vehicle', although I would have assumed this was self-evident. (c. 1905)

PEACE CELEBRATIONS AT HOREHAM ROAD were held at Constance Scott's field in July 1923. Among those enjoying the carnival atmosphere in the fancy dress competition are Frank Hobday and Mr Nye as policeman and convict, while Frank Piper is the country yokel. Constance Scott presented the recreation ground to the parish in 1938.

A FETE was held on the day the Constance Scott Recreation Ground was given to the village. Fred Goldsmith (with the whip) and Bill Barnes won the competition for the best turned-out wagon and team. Note the decorative bells, only worn on special occasions. The speeches were delivered from the Sussex wagon. (1938)

THE WORKSHOP OF A.G. PHILLIPS & SONS, builders, was situated on the road adjacent to the station entrance, opposite the Corn Stores. The firm was responsible for building Kingston Villas and houses along Chiddingly Road and Manor Road. Left to right: Sydney Delves, Albert (Bun) Phillips, Ben Phillips. (*c*. 1925)

FERNYHOUGH'S LIBRARY with the adjoining Horeham Road post office, as it appeared in *c*. 1910 when Ernest Lemon was the sub-postmaster. This is one of several sites in Horam where the village post office stood, prior to its arrival at the current High Street site. This building is now the site of Read's Garage on Little London Road. The house alongside is now sadly derelict.

BURNT HOUSE FARM near Tanners Manor has extensive views across open land towards Horeham Road. It may have been much more physically demanding work to plough a field with a cart horse and hand-held plough but it is certainly more photogenic than its modern motorized equivalent. (*c.* 1930)

A MOTOR CAR TAKES THE BEND at Sharps Corner, leading out of Horeham Road towards Little London, with the turning to Lions Green alongside the finger-post.

SECTION EIGHT

Maynards Green

LOOKING NORTH ALONG THE MAIN ROAD, with the wall of Maynards Green School on the left. Notice how the original gateway has been bricked in as it was no longer safe to have an exit for chidren on the Tubwell Lane corner once motorized traffic had increased. A particularly ornate telephone kiosk stood opposite, with William Delves's general store to its left, which sold everything from food and clothing to animal foodstuffs. It even had its own bakehouse at the rear. (*c.* 1935)

A 'GOSPEL CARAVAN' is being towed past Maynards Green School on its way to its next venue. When itinerant preachers visited rural communities like Maynards Green, they would usually stay for a week and set up their caravans on land belonging to one of the local congregation. The Model N Standard Fordson tractor has long rear wings which were shortened during war production to economize on the use of metal. (*c.* 1936)

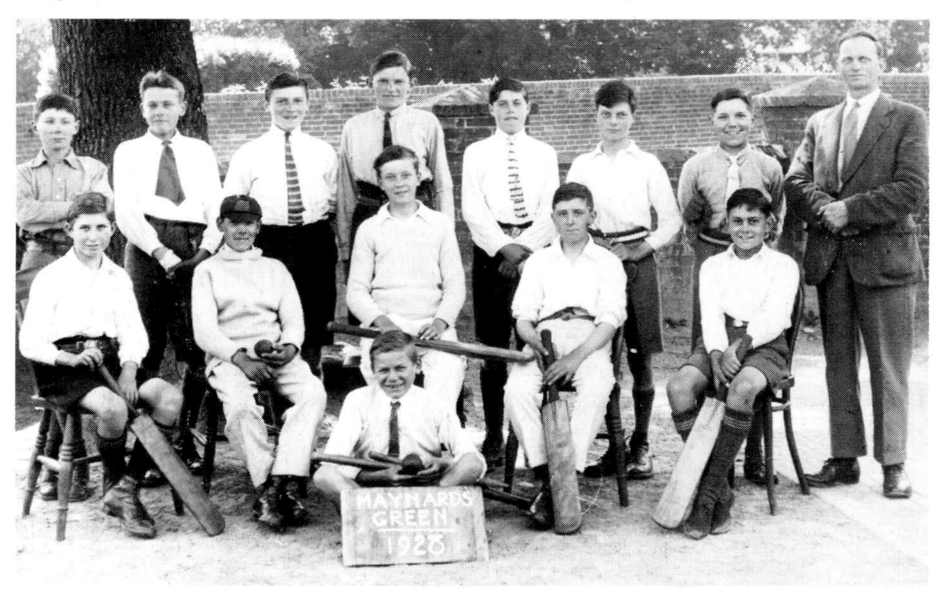

MAYNARDS GREEN SCHOOL CRICKET TEAM in 1928 include (standing): Ron Thompson, Prowy Morris, Fred Tickner, Marcus Piper, Fred Winkler, Alan Ashby, George Foord, Mr A. Robinson. Seated: Ron Piper, Clarence Relf, Harold Smith, Charles Westgate, Arthur Venus. On floor: Frank Dumbrill.

BEEKEEPING CLUB AT MAYNARDS GREEN SCHOOL in the 1920s. Headmaster James Jervis looks on as the pupils, among them Sydney Delves, John Longhurst and Fred Nye, inspect a honeycomb at close quarters and receive instruction from county bee expert Mr Kenward.

WHAT AN EASY WAY TO GET YOUR GARDENING DONE! Unfortunately it only works if you are the headmaster and can co-opt a large team of less than willing schoolboys to do all the work for you. Here, at Maynards Green School, the boys not only have to dig the garden, but also mow the lawn and then roll it.

FOOTPRINTS TESTIFY TO THE DEPTH OF THE SNOW at the bottom of West Street Lane, where a bridge crosses Waldron Gill, in February 1934. Rumary's Cottage stands on the right, immediately in front of the Tubwell Lane junction.

A BEAUTIFUL POSED STUDY of three elderly ladies in their bonnets and lace outside their cottage on Tubwell Lane.

SECTION NINE

Little London

FRANK PIPER leans proudly against his Penny Farthing bicycle in *c.* 1890. The radius of its front wheel was 54 in, it had solid tyres, precarious balance and no brakes; yet Frank would regularly ride up and down New Pond Hill. At the time he was working as an assistant at Neves in Heathfield.

THE CANNON HOUSE at Little London is a reminder of the importance of the iron industry – and the manufacturing of weaponry – to this area of the Sussex Weald. Even the village sign has a cannon incorporated into its design. A small amount of ancient cinder (slag left after iron smelting) has been found at Stony field, suggesting there was a bloomery or burning site in the vicinity, although obviously not as large as the furnaces at Waldron or Old Heathfield. (*c.* 1910)

THE COTTAGE, viewed from across the triangle of grass which is actually part of its garden and not the village green. In the 1930s it was bought by Dr Woods, a Harley Street psychiatrist, as a weekend home. He also bought The Cannon House, which he transformed into a small nursing home for wealthy private patients with mental disorders, and Link Cottage, as a home for his cook and his gardener. After the fire which gutted The Cannon House, the patients had to move into The Cottage. (1914)

THE CANNON HOUSE was gutted by fire during 1940, not through enemy action but due to a smouldering beam in the chimney. By the time that the National Fire Service at Heathfield had been contacted, the fire had already caused extensive damage to the roof. It broke out in the early hours of the morning and the nurses and patients had to climb out of upstairs windows using sheets tied together to make their escape.

LOCAL MEMBERS OF THE WARTIME NATIONAL FIRE SERVICE from Heathfield inspect the charred remains of an attic bedroom at The Cannon House: Reg Ford, Ken Angood, Ernie Phillips and, with head showing in the bottom corner, Jack Neve.

FRANK PIPER'S GENERAL STORE AND POST OFFICE, as it appeared before structural alterations in 1924. After leaving Neves Bros. Frank set up a post office business at Fairview for a number of years, before buying this building in *c.* 1905 and converting it from a 'Snob's' (a bootmaker's shop) into a general store. Among items stocked were two-gallon cans of petrol. (*c.* 1910)

HOSPITAL SUNDAY in *c.* 1927. The annual procession, with accompanying bands and banners, would set off from Horam and pause at Little London for tea before turning down the by-road to Tanners Manor where a service would be held. Collection boxes would raise funds for the Eastbourne hospitals. Here part of the procession forms up under the banner of the Tunbridge Wells Equitable Friendly Society outside Frank Piper's shop. He stands on the left, in sash, rosette and trilby, and was treasurer of the organization.

THE TWO WOODHEY COTTAGES, on the right, were built in *c.* 1915 by Frank Piper. With the invention of hand-cranked petrol pumps, Frank Piper decided to expand his business interests and set up a filling station alongside the shop. The Piper family continued to operate both the shop and the petrol station until they were sold to Salvidge's in 1967. (*c.* 1935)

TE-WHARE HOTEL was set on the west side of the main road to the south of the hamlet. The bungalow on the left was built in 1906 and given the name Te-Whare, which means 'homestead' in Maori. The hotel was expanded with a second bungalow on the right and finally an extension was built which joined the two. A further building was later added as a tea room at the bottom of the lawn and tennis court. The hotel was closed in the 1960s and divided into separate dwellings. (*c.* 1925)

FERN COTTAGE, next to The Spinney School, in *c.* 1890. Standing outside is local woodman Thomas Piper who worked in Broad Wood. He was later (1903) to buy Fern Cottage – together with a pigsty opposite – for £130. A small extension has since been added on the right.

THE LANE BETWEEN LITTLE LONDON AND WALDRON has no officially designated name, despite this postcard's original caption 'Waldron Road'. Brooklyn (now known as Clare Cottage) was built in the 1880s and given the name because of the tiny stream in the garden. It sits alongside a small triangle of grass at a junction of small country lanes. In the distance on the left Glaziers Farm can be seen. (*c.* 1920)

SECTION TEN

Waldron

A VICTORIAN CABINET-SIZED PHOTOGRAPH of the wide expanse of roadway which used to be the village green. On the right is the sixteenth-century Star Inn. Is it a hitching post for horses which runs along the front? Ebenezer Daw's general store, with a telegraph pole alongside, has not yet extended to the left. It had its own bakehouse to the rear. (*c.* 1880)

WALDRON'S STAR INN has stood on this site since 1620. Inside there is a beautiful inglenook fireplace with a locally produced iron fireback dated 1694. Directly behind the War Memorial is the outbuilding which has, at various times, been used as the village post office.

THE UNVEILING OF WALDRON'S WAR MEMORIAL in the middle of the village green on 25 July 1920. The military guard of honour are reversing their arms as a sign of respect to those parishioners who died in the First World War.

A HORSE-DRAWN DELIVERY CART for Ebenezer Daw's general stores, which used to occupy the prime position on the village green. (Yes, it was once a green, with a finger-post pointing out directions and distances.) The Daw family were local entrepreneurs, with various members of the family setting up general stores in many of the villages in the area in the early years of this century. (*c*. 1919)

ERNEST CHEEK inside the village forge where he worked for more than forty of his fifty-five years as a blacksmith. With the decline in the number of horses which needed to be shod, he increasingly concentrated his business on making decorative ironwork and repairing agricultural implements. For a while at the turn of the century, when Albert Dawes was the blacksmith, the village post office moved into the left area of the forge. More recently the post office occupied the single-storey building next door to the smithy.

CROSS FARM before its dormer windows and grand gateway were added. The Tithe Barn was built in the eleventh century and it is possible that the original farm building was contemporary. The current brick building was erected in 1622 by the Hammonds, the ironmasters and tanners. Since 1979 St George's Vineyard has been established here. (*c.* 1910)

NELSON KENWAY FARMED HOPS AT CROSS FARM and increasingly produced his own beer, which was stored in a cave in The Rocks. He also operated a successful off-licence on Heathfield High Street. The misnamed 'coal tree' is more correctly bog oak, lignite formed by the preservative qualities of the acidic bog. Some of the well-seasoned wood was used to make oak panelling within Cross Farm, but I have also been assured that the lych gate at All Saints' church (built in memory of Louis Huth of Possingworth) was constructed out of this particular tree trunk.

THE BELFRY OF ALL SAINTS', Waldron, contains a peal of eight bells (all cast and dated from 1732 to 1780). Two of them were recast by John Warner in 1887 to commemorate Queen Victoria's Jubilee. In 1912 all the bells were sent to John Warner's Spitalfields Bell Foundry in north-east London to be recast. The illustration shows them at the foundry.

'THE WHITE COONS OF WALDRON'. I am sure the Commission For Racial Equality would no longer allow any singing troupe to perform under this somewhat paradoxical name, but then public sensitivity on this issue had not yet been raised. As they have not blacked up their faces and have chosen to dress in Pierrot costumes it seems an even stranger name. Presumably these early forerunners of the Martlets are performing at a local garden party.

THOSE WERE THE DAYS – in this postcard there are three different shops in view! The Queen Anne cottages on the left used to house a sweet shop, later a general store. The cottages were demolished in 1975 because they were frequently flooded as their earth floors were below the road level. Alongside was the butcher's shop of Roger's & Son (now the general store and post office – and the last surviving village shop). Behind the tree on the right can be seen the post office sign on the front of Charlie Humphrey's shop.

LOOKING ALONG THE STREET when it was a place of rural charm and tranquility, with no traffic or pedestrians in sight. The Street still presents an interesting variety of old and attractive houses and cottages for the visitor to view. (c. 1914)

LOOKING EAST ALONG WALDRON STREET from the corner of Glebe Field at the junction with North Street. The newly-erected wooden palings on the right stood outside Lucas Memorial Hall, which had been recently built in 1904. (c. 1906)

LUCAS MEMORIAL HALL was built by Joseph Lucas of Foxhunt Manor in 1904 and presented to the village after the death of his wife. At various times it has served as the village hall and the local reading room. Note the terra cotta coat of arms of Foxhunt built into the brickwork.

THE OLD MANOR HOUSE AT FOXHUNT to the south of Waldron dates back to medieval times when it was known as The Scrip. At the time of writing, planning permission is being sought to develop the land around into an eighteen hole golf course.

THE LODGE TO FOXHUNT MANOR, here with a broken gate, does little to suggest the magnificence of the edifice set way out of sight up the long private driveway. The lodge, with its terra cotta plaque dated 1897, guards the new gateway at the entrance to the drive which leads up to the Convent of the Visitation.

FOXHUNT MANOR was built in red brick by Joseph Lucas in 1898, apparently to the same design as another he had already built in France. By 1936 the Xaverian Brotherhood had transformed it into a seminary for young men training for the priesthood. In 1960 a closed order of Carmelite nuns adopted it as their home: the Convent of the Visitation. The tennis courts have, not surprisingly therefore, now gone; the ivy no longer grows up the façade; and the chimney pots have been cut off after six were blown down in the 1987 hurricane force winds.

A CHAUFFEUR-DRIVEN DAIMLER parks at the main entrance to Foxhunt Manor. While most of the building is constructed in red brick, many of the architectural details such as the battlement crenellations and the window mouldings are made of terra cotta – apparently the cheapest material at the time. The conservatory is still in position but a new porch entrance has been added.

TANNERS MANOR at Lions Green is thought to have derived its name from the nearby tanyard. It was originally built as a traditional Elizabethan E-shaped house but was later rebuilt in stone in the Jacobean period. Major structural alterations have taken place over the centuries, e.g. the demolition of two of its wings, but another wing has been added on the left even since this 1910 photograph, which was taken from the bottom of the drive. Many eminent names have been connected with Tanners Manor: Sir Philip Sydney; Roger, Earl of Rutland; the Sackville family; the Fullers (who developed the iron industry in this area); the Bonnicks; and, since 1898, the Hassells.

MR BENDEN SHARVELL HASSELL sits proudly in front of Uckfield's horse-drawn fire-tender and its team of volunteer firemen. The photograph is believed to have been taken in the grounds of Tanners Manor in *c.* 1910. As a local benefactor, he had Waldron's cricket pitch levelled and had the cricket pavilion erected in memory of his brother, Col. Bray Hassell, JP

HOSPITAL SUNDAY in c. 1927. This was one of the major annual fund-raising events for the Eastbourne hospitals, which serviced the medical needs of this locality. Most local organizations and Friendly Societies would march behind their banners, to the accompaniment of the local silver bands, along the roads and lanes from Horeham Road, to Little London and finally to Tanners Manor where an outdoor service was held.

HOUSES AND LAND FOR SALE

bordering the Park and enjoying the views illustrated.

Further particulars from the resident Estate Agent, Possingworth Park Estate Office (Phone Heatfield 282).
All houses and sites have electric light, main water and gas. Sites from £100 to £500 per acre. Houses from £1000 to £6000 Specially designed to your personal requirements, but we usually have several ready for immediate occupation, write as below and ask for booklet. P. 137

LIONS GREEN

HORAM — Telephone Horeham Road 14. — EAST SUSSEX.

AN ADVERTISEMENT TO LURE PEOPLE TO LIONS GREEN in c. 1939. Lions Green houses were built to a high standard and sometimes to individual specifications. Even today estate agencies will advertise a property as a 'Lions Green-type house' because this is synonymous with individuality and quality in design.

ONE OF SUSSEX'S LAST WORKING OX-TEAMS was to be found at Possingworth. The illustration shows a team of six yoked oxen drawing a binder – presumably over very heavy ground. Driving these thick-skinned and sometimes stubborn creatures required a goad, a tipped stick, rather than a whip, which they would often ignore. (1905)

WHAT A SUBJECT FOR A POSTCARD! I think you might be in danger of losing a friend if you sent this postcard, originally captioned 'manure carting', with the standard 'Wish you were here' message. Notice the very thick wheel rims on the ox-drawn manure cart to enable it to be pulled across very muddy ground or the local soft clay. (1905)

SECTION ELEVEN

Cross in Hand

A MEET OF THE FOXHOUNDS AND THE HUNT outside Alfred Seamer's Cross in Hand Hotel in c. 1905. Eventually so many farmers and smallholders kept poultry that it became impractical for any foxhounds to hunt in the area, so shoots had to be organized to cull the number of foxes.

CROSS IN HAND HOTEL has stood on this site, dominating the junction, for many centuries, with some of the earlier features of the building dating back to *c.* 1600, although it is predominantly *c.* 1700. The Seamer family ran the hotel from 1883 until 1970. The stables alongside were later transformed into a petrol station by R.A. Pither. The blur in the centre shows the problem of long exposure times for early photographs. (*c.* 1895)

THE WOODEN WORKSHOP on the extreme right is that of Jarvis's, for many generations a firm of builders and undertakers.. It is always surprising to see just how many small businesses – and shops in particular – were able to flourish in even a comparatively small centre of population like Cross in Hand until the early years of this century.

THE TURNPIKE ROAD FROM BURWASH TO LEWES was established in 1765. To collect the tolls which were levied, toll cottages were built alongside the pay gates. The white cottage on the left was Cross in Hand's pay gate and later became the bicycle repair workshop of Horace Thorpe. Next door stands the village general store of W.S. Burt.

A SIMILAR VIEW taken about ten years later showing the general store of W.S. Burt on the left. On the right can be seen James Herring's bakery. His shop was the single-storey brick-built structure which fronted onto the main Mayfield Road. Although it has long been demolished, its position can be seen on the side wall of the Corner House. The bakery moved to Albion House in 1904. The white weatherboarded building next along was the builder's workshop of Albert Jarvis, with the top of its external wooden staircase just visible. Jarvis's has operated on this site since *c.* 1880.

LOOKING ALONG THE MAIN ROAD with Mrs Amelia James Saunders' shop on the right. It served as a tobacconist's and also the village post office and telegraph office. Today there is a mower repair shop here.

A DELIVERY BICYCLE leans against the railings outside Southdown House, then the butcher's shop of Henry Ticehurst and Edward Thurston. (It has remained a butcher's, now P. & I. Hobden.) A baker's cart stands outside Albion House, then James Herring's bakery, with its bakehouse set behind. His original bakery had been at the Corner House until Albion House was built for him in 1904. It continues to be a bakery.

ALMA VILLA stands on the left, beside A. Burtenshaw's posters giving auction details for Firle, Hurstmonceux, Ashburnham and Ninfield. Further along on the left is the office of Robert Jarvis, the undertaker, who took over when his father died in 1909.

LOOKING NORTH ALONG THE LEWES ROAD towards the Methodist church which was erected in 1896. A small child sits on the triangle of grass, alongside the lane which leads up to the windmill. Close inspection of A.D. Hobden's bread delivery cart shows that it is probably a type of three-wheeled delivery cycle. The cottage on the left has long gone, while the large house behind it, with a splendid monkey puzzle tree in its garden, used to serve as a local hostelry and coaching house. (*c.* 1910)

CROSS IN HAND'S TWO WINDMILLS were both operated by the long-lasting partnership of the Newnham and Ashdown families. The Old Mill, a post-mill with four sweeps, had apparently survived from *c.* 1776 but, by 1900, it had become rather unsafe and was demolished soon afterwards. Two of its sweeps were sent to Dicker New Mill and other parts to Blackboys Mill. Its roundhouse, however, was retained and is still in its original position. It is recorded that an old travelling woman was struck by one of the sweeps in 1843 and killed. (*c.* 1900)

DO YOUR POULTRY PAY ? ? ?

If not, buy from **NEWNHAM & ASHDOWN,** the old established firm, who have stood the test for over 40 years.

CORN, SUSSEX GROUND OATS and MASHES of the best quality supplied. All orders receive prompt attention.

AN ADVERTISING POSTCARD offering publicity for the produce of Newnham and Ashdown's windmill at Cross in Hand. The partnership was established in 1888 and was a major supplier of foodstuffs for the flourishing local chicken industry in particular. (*c.* 1930)

CROSS IN HAND'S NEW MILL originally stood at Mount Ephraim (Framfield) and was moved to Cross in Hand by oxen in 1855. It was later moved to its present site in 1868. Despite the ravages of the weather, for example the structural damage caused by the gales of October 1932, it remained working until 1969, when a stock broke. The mill was the largest post-mill in Sussex and was also the last working windmill in the county.

CROSS IN HAND USED TO HAVE A YOUTH HOSTEL. It was built in 1932 across the lane from the windmill but had to be closed at the beginning of the Second World War when it was occupied by Canadian troops. Their behaviour was sometimes so troublesome that some villagers commented they would have preferred to have had German POWs staying there. The hostel has now been converted into two dwellings. (*c.* 1932)

A CARRIER'S CART makes a delivery along Beaconsfield Terrace in *c*. 1910, while the postman walks slowly past.

LOOKING UP THE HILL OF FIRGROVE ROAD towards the Methodist church, with Victoria Cottages on the right and Salisbury Terrace and Beaconsfield Terrace on the left. This area of Cross in Hand was developed immediately after the building of the church in 1896. (c. 1918)

LOOKING ALONG FIRGROVE ROAD towards Cross in Hand, just north of where Warren Road joins at Roser's Cross.

REAPERS AT HOLMES HILL FARM REST AFTER THEIR LABOURS, while children sit at their feet amidst the stubble. A variety of tools are on show. Several of the men carry serrated edged sickles, while the two on the right carry a flail and a crate-scythe. I wonder what liquid refreshment is in the stone jar: something alcoholic, or perhaps some fizzy drink locally produced by Thomas Foord on New Pond Hill?

THE NEW POND at the bottom of New Pond Hill was in fact an artificial lake with its own boathouse. It used to be part of the Heatherden estate. Its water level was controlled by a series of sluice gates and this was fed through to the watermill on the opposite side of the road. The lake was always well stocked with fish and in the depths of winter it was used as the local skating rink.

THE FOORD FAMILY BOUGHT A PLOT OF LAND on New Pond Hill in 1848 and built a beautiful cottage, Homestalls (visible on the right), with an adjoining dairy. Here they produced ginger beer for their own consumption and then started selling it locally. By 1880 Thomas Foord, the son, was a successful businessman, marketing all manner of fizzy drinks. (*c.* 1920)

PINE GARAGE, on Little London Road, was originally a barn converted into a car repair workshop by Horace Thorpe, who had earlier dealt in bicycles alongside the Cross in Hand Hotel. He was rather an eccentric character and, in his desire to be able to view the sea, he had the strange projection built into the roof of the garage as a viewing platform. By the time of this photograph his son Ron was the proprietor.

CROWDS GATHER TO CELEBRATE the laying of the foundation stone of the church hall for St Bartholomew's by Mrs A.W. Morris of Culverwood on 15 September 1931. It was built on a plot of land on the Sheepsetting Lane junction, alongside Thorpe's Garage.

LOOKING DOWN THE SNOW COVERED HILL OF LITTLE LONDON ROAD in *c*. 1910, with Cross in Hand School behind the railings on the right. The left side of the road is still heavily wooded and not yet developed.

A BUILDING GANG poses outside Cross in Hand School in 1908, presumably after adding a small extension.

CROSS IN HAND'S FIRST NATIONAL SCHOOL was opened at what is now Church Cottage in 1876 but a new purpose-built school was erected across the road in c. 1899 with D.J. Holt as the first headmaster. A new infants room was added in 1914. It was closed in 1985 and demolished soon afterwards.

MR DAVID JOHN HOLT was the first headmaster of the new Cross in Hand School and served in that capacity until 1918. He was apparently a firm disciplinarian and was actively involved in the musical life of St Bartholomew's church where he was organist and choirmaster. He was also the owner of a magnificent early motor bicycle.

THE JUNCTION WITH LITTLE LONDON ROAD was once adorned with a telephone kiosk for the Automobile Association, often supervised by patrolman Mr Garlick. On the right can be seen the lodge for Heatherden (built in *c.* 1860 for J.C. Boucher, who gave St Bartholomew's church to the parish) and, further along, Church Cottage, which was Cross in Hand's first National School, from 1876 until 1898.

A VIEW ACROSS OPEN HEATHLAND towards a rather distant Tilsmore recreation ground (given to the parish of Cross in Hand at the end of the First World War). The field to the north of the main road (hidden in the tree-lined valley) had been part of George Berry's market garden until this time. Today the sloping heathland is covered by the houses of Pages Close, while the recreation ground is the site of Nursery Way. (*c.* 1920)

A PLATOON OF SCOTTISH INFANTRY march along Mount Pleasant in 1938, while their officers ride along more comfortably at the rear of the column. The drone of the bagpipes has brought local inhabitants to their upstairs windows to watch.

HORSE-DRAWN TROOPS are overtaken by a Southdown double-decker omnibus near the bottom of Pages Hill on 26 August 1933.

THE ANNUAL HORSE SHOW, the highlight of the social calendar at Cross in Hand, was held every August on what are now the Hardy Roberts playing fields but which were than part of the Heatherden estate. Marquees and grandstands would be set up for the large crowds who would attend. There is certainly a magnificent range of bonnets on view in the grandstand. (1910)

ACTIVITIES AT THE HORSE SHOW extended to a large range of horse competitions, including jumping, trotting, working horses and more unusual ones like troika racing (the troika is a Russian carriage drawn by three horses riding abreast). (1910)

CUPS AND PRIZES would be awarded by the guest of honour to the winner of each competition. (1910)

CROSS IN HAND HORSE SHOW became increasingly commercialized as it became successful. In its prime, travelling fairs such as Pettigrews would attend with their sideshows, rides and roundabouts. The following day was declared Children's Day, with all the fun of the fair – including a tea – free for the local children. (1920)

AN EARLY ROAD ACCIDENT near Possingworth in 1911. Charlie Ryder stands on top of an overturned Daimler, attempting to turn it upright by means of lifting tackle attached to a giant set of shear-legs.

SCHOOL BUS DRAMA when a Southdown double-decker bus, horribly overloaded with pupils celebrating the last day of the Easter term at Lewes County Grammar Schools, swerved to avoid an oncoming furniture van and toppled down a ten-foot embankment into a ploughed field north of Sharlands crossroads. Five Heathfield students were detained in hospital after the accident. (1952)

CROSS IN HAND'S CRICKET TEAM played host to a benefit match in honour of John Langridge, the Sussex player, on the Hardy Roberts playing field on Saturday 12 September 1953. Three internationals played in the John Langridge XI: his brother James, G. Doggart and the Revd David Sheppard. Standing left to right: -?-, -?-, John Langridge, D. Manville, Charlie Oakes, V. Leveridge, B. Geall, Ron Poulton (captain of Cross in Hand), Les Lenham, Henry Mackay, Bill Kemp, Revd David Sheppard, Ken Hook, Roy Ticehurst, E.C. Cuss, Bill Smith, George Cox, James Langridge, G. Doggart, Jack Burgess, H. Durrant (umpire). Squatting: Geoff Newnham, Dennis Sinden.

ISENHURST TENNIS CLUB in 1936. The smiling faces and the suggestion of an 'Anyone for tennis?' attitude make them look like they are all auditioning for parts in *The Boy Friend*.

ISENHURST MANOR, in its ivy-clad prime, really was a magnificent looking property, with its well-laid out ornamental lawns. The name is derived from the Old English for 'Iron Wood', suggesting that iron-smelting was taking place in this area in medieval times. (1908)

THE LODGE COTTAGE for the Isenhurst Estate guards the ornamental gateway to the east of the main road leading to Five Ashes. (1908)

SECTION TWELVE

Five Ashes

A CHARMING POSTCARD VIEW of the village taken from the Green in *c.* 1908, showing the range of vehicular transport available at this period: from bicycles to horse-drawn carts and carriages and with an early car parked on the forecourt of the Five Ashes Inn (with its five pollarded lime trees clearly visible). The village school in the distance was built in 1872 when local children had to pay 2d. per week to attend.

THE TRIANGULAR GREEN at Five Ashes before the War Memorial was erected. On the small area of grass on the other side of the white marker posts the game of quoits was played. The house overlooking the quoits bed is, not surprisingly, called Quoits Cottage. (1916)

A FUSILADE OF SHOTS is fired into the air in memory of the villagers who died during the First World War, as part of the dedication service of the War Memorial on the village green on 18 June 1920. The upper part of the stone memorial was destroyed by the hurricane force winds which caused havoc throughout the county in October 1987 and a new War Memorial (with a metal cross) was re-dedicated on 13 November 1988.

LOCAL WORKMEN pose as road repairs are carried out at Summer Hill in 1925. The strange tool in the centre is a boning rod. (Several rods would be lined up with their posts sunk to a certain depth. When the tops of the Ts were seen to be level, the depth to be dug could now be ascertained.) Note the particularly broad wheel rim of the Sussex wagon – necessary because of the soft local clay.

HOP PICKING AT DOG KENNEL LANE in 1921. Posed around the hessian hop bin are standing, from left to right: F. Bassett, C. Bassett, D. Barden, Mrs Barden, Mrs Bellingham, Mrs Smith, ? Smith, 'Frog's Spit' a local gipsy character. Seated: B. Barden, ? Smith, ? Smith.

TWITTS GHYLL (originally Twitts Farm) is an L-shaped sixteenth-century timber-framed Sussex farmhouse, partly rebuilt in brick. It lies to the north of Butcher's Cross at the junction of what is now Fir Toll Road. It was for many years the home of the famous politician Sir Austen Chamberlain who was Chancellor of the Exchequer in 1903 and Foreign Secretary during the 1920s.

CRABB FARM is one of many listed buildings in the environs of Five Ashes. It was built in the seventeenth century with the ground floor of red brick and grey headers and with the upper floor tile hung. It has been much altered over the years and even by the time of this *c.* 1910 postcard, when the land was farmed by William Ness, the farmhouse had been converted into two cottages.

SECTION THIRTEEN

Mayfield

A GENERAL PANORAMA OF MAYFIELD, taken from the south, shows clearly how the High Street follows the ridge along the skyline. Of particular interest is the group of white single-storey buildings to the right. These belonged to the strict community of Anglican nuns of St Mary's in the Field. Here they ran an orphanage where they encouraged the boys, on leaving, to emigrate to New Zealand to become sheep farmers while the girls were allowed to remain local. In the centre, with a dark roof, stood Tom Geer's Old Brew House, an alehouse and 'doss house', where you could sleep on the floor on a straw palliasse for 2d. (1p) per night. (1930)

LOOKING DOWN WELLBROOK HILL in 1930, along the deceptively dangerous stretch of road which often resembles a race track nowadays. The local Tenants Association have yet to build the final block of four cottages at Rothermead (added 1933) while the houses on Berkeley Road, just this side of the bridge over the River Rother, would not be built until 1936. The pair of slate cottages on the right were demolished in 1971.

AN AERIAL VIEW OF THE RAILWAY STATION in c. 1930. The wide approach of Station Road (formerly The Level) can be clearly distinguished, leading to the station itself and the goods yard. The main road from Five Ashes (now the A267) is difficult to spot as it runs from bottom centre, past Bill Brown's market garden and Sivyer's builder's yard, before reaching the corner site of the Station Hotel, with Mist Cottages diametrically opposite. Leading off left after the rail bridge is Fir Toll Road – originally Twitts Ghyll Road.

RAILWAY HOTEL. Unlike at Heathfield and Horeham Road where the arrival of the railway station transformed the villages beyond recognition, at Mayfield very little apparent change and no massive developments in houses and shops took place near the station. One obvious newcomer, however, was the Railway Hotel, built to accommodate rail travellers. In this *c.* 1910 advertising postcard, when Alfred Savage was landlord, a carriage (with a top-hatted coachman) waits patiently for a customer while a milk-cart delivers to the rear.

THE VIEW UP THE HILL near the Railway Hotel leads past Mist (or sometimes Miss) Cottages, which take their name from the medieval family of Nicholas Le Mist.

MAYFIELD RAILWAY STATION, with its distinctive decorative canopy and the two-storey station-master's house, stood on the 'Down' platform, with a pedestrian underpass at its far end allowing access to the opposite platform. Looking along the 'Up' platform in this *c.* 1882 photograph, the original LB & SCR signal box (dismantled *c.* 1931), with a small waiting room further along, can be seen. As elsewhere on the Cuckoo Line, there were two rail tracks within the vicinity of the station itself.

A GENERAL VIEW of the exterior of Mayfield railway station as seen from Love Lane. To the left is the station building, with its station-master's house. To the right is the goods yard with the goods warehouse behind. Further to the right stood the coal bunkers and the animal pens.

TOOTH'S BANK DERAILMENT on 1 September 1897 caused the only fatality during the eighty-five years of the Cuckoo Line's existence, when D1 class 0–4–2 tank locomotive No. 297 *Bonchurch* left the track and toppled to its right while approaching Mayfield along the sharply curving gradient near Clayton Farm, killing driver James McKinley. Five of the six carriages were thrown down the embankment on the left, injuring many passengers. In this damaged photograph, D3 class No. 381 *Fittleworth* has brought up the inspection team to view the wreckage.

TWO SNAPSHOTS OF THE LAYING OF THE NEW TRACK at Tooth's Bank which replaced that damaged in the 1897 derailment. (The old single-line track can be seen behind.) The Accident Report recommended that speed be reduced on this stretch of track and that a further two minutes be timetabled for the Heathfield–Mayfield journey. Another of the contributory causes was that the outside rail on the curve was not banked to the desired $2\frac{1}{2}$ in, after heavy rain had caused settlement of the ground underneath.

A TRAIN of the London, Brighton & South Coast Railway (No. 2) approaches the bridge, often called the Echo Arch, close to the Love Lane/Rotherfield Lane junction in *c.* 1920. A road now follows the course of the old line at this point.

WHILE THE NATURAL GAS FIELDS OF ENGLAND LTD were exploiting the discovery of Natural Gas at Heathfield, they were also doing exploratory drilling at two sites in Mayfield. This rare illustration shows an exploratory bore-hole on the site of the coal yard at the railway station, with Love Lane running along the top of the embankment. (1902)

MAYFIELD BONFIRE BOYS AND BELLES, including several of the Carpenter, Fenner and Easton families, in a strange selection of patriotic costumes, including John Bull, Britannia and various military and naval uniforms. (*c.* 1905)

ONE OF THE FLOATS at Mayfield's bonfire carnival on 5 November 1936. It was driven by H. Morley and steered by D. Bellingham. Dressed as nurses on the float are J. Roser and F. Eaton, while Messrs Lusted (his son is the patient with the broken arm), E. Carpenter and S. Foard are clad in chain mail.

LOOKING ALONG WEST STREET, with the entrance to Cranesden on the right. It was once a beautiful ancient farmhouse but is now considerably enlarged. It once served as the refuge for the Puritan vicar of Mayfield, John Maynard, when he was ousted from his post in 1662. To the left can be seen Schoolhouse Cottages, although no-one seems to know to which local school they were linked. (c. 1935)

SNOW ADDS TO THE PICTURESQUE CHARM of West Street – formerly known as the Lower Level – as we look up the hill towards the South Street and High Street junctions. Note the pub sign of the Sawyer's Arms hanging outside Shirley House and the corner site of the Plough – two of several inns in Mayfield to have ceased trading as licensed premises during this century.

THE PARTICULAR BAPTIST CHAPEL as it appeared several years after the building of the present chapel in 1873 on the junction of South Street and West Street. There has been a long history of Independent worship in the Mayfield area so it was built with a seating capacity of 250. However, church-going has ceased to be regarded as such an essential element of village life, and congregation sizes have dwindled considerably. (*c.* 1880)

SOUTH STREET is the pretty, open street set below the level of the High Street but parallel to it. An Austin 7 parks outside Holly Cottage. Next along are the open doors of the workshop at the rear of Rogers, now all boarded up. New houses have recently filled the gap where the high wall stands. The van in the distance is a Raleigh 3-wheeler and opposite it stood a granary. On the right of the photographer was the site of the Brewer's Arms. (*c.* 1945)

LEWES OLD BANK had its Mayfield branch built by Lesters on the High Street site which had long been occupied by Albert Foard's shoemaker's shop. The building is actually four storeys high since a cellar had to be built as the bank vault. The building on the left, once an old forge, was, at the time of this photograph, a sweet shop and tobacconist's run by Mrs Cottingham, whose husband George was a blacksmith on South Street. This was also Mayfield's first telephone exchange, before it moved to the site of the Plough on West Street. (1909)

LOOKING WEST towards the West Street junction with its horse trough, erected in memory of J.J. Tylor in 1901. By the turn of the century Barclays Bank had absorbed the Sussex-based Lewes Old Bank and later Gordon Rogers was to set up his business in the house alongside.

WHAT A STRANGE COMBINATION OF BUSINESSES for one family to run in the same building (now a dwelling house). Gordon Rogers sold bicycles and accessories in the left-hand section and also set up a repair workshop for pedal and motor bicycles down the passage alongside on Back Lane. His wife Emily sold embroidery and drapery. (The business was later to be the first in Mayfield to deal in radios and televisions.) The upstairs window also advertises ladies hairdressing.

JOSEPH CORNFORD first established a dairy business in the front of this dwelling-house on the High Street before expanding it into a general grocery store. Miss Celia Cornford poses in the doorway. Next door stood Florence's, a ladies' hairdresser. (*c.* 1935)

APRONED STAFF pose outside the open doorway of the Star. It was demolished in c. 1920 after considerable fire damage, and Sivyer Bros. built their Central Garage on the site. The Star's liquor licence was transferred to the Middle House which became a licensed inn only at this time.

STONE COURT was built in the fourteenth century, probably as a thatched farmhouse. Since then it has served as an alehouse, in 1641 Mayfield's Poor House (with looms and spinning in the attic), a Reading Room, in 1890 a School of Woodcarving and Gilding, and, in this c. 1920 postcard, Mayfield Conservative Club. It is now a private residence but Fenners run a shop at the front.

GEORGE V's CORONATION in May 1937 has brought out the celebratory flags and bunting at Sivyer Bros.' Central Garage (on the High Street) and the adjoining tea shop, 'The Old Star Cellar' of H.M. Smith. The beautiful half-timbered frontage – so in keeping with the historical charm of Mayfield – is in fact a 1920s' reconstruction. To the left can be seen the newspaper adverts outside Fenners, the local newsagent and colour merchant.

THE INTERIOR OF SIVYER BROS.' GARAGE reveals the rather soulless reconstruction behind the beautiful façade of the building – albeit, a practical and economical use of the space as a car showroom and for automobile repairs. Sivyers were the local agents for Austin and Morris cars and sold petrol on the very narrow forecourt. Visible through the open doorway is the old shop front of Fenners the tailors.

A DELIVERY IS MADE to the Royal Oak Hotel by Alfred Fenner's horse-drawn carrier's cart, which operated from the railway station. Jim Bale, in his leather apron, stands chatting on the footpath while further along can be seen the uniformed telegraph boy. Second-hand furniture is on display outside Edward Napper's furniture shop. He also did business as an ironmonger, blacksmith and farmer. (*c.* 1908)

A CHARMING STUDY of the relative peace and tranquility to be found along Mayfield High Street in the Edwardian days when motorized transport was still a rarity. Children could walk or skip along the middle of the road with nothing speedier than Fenner's delivery cart to be wary of. The beautifully half-timbered Middle House, built in 1576, was still a private residence at this time. (*c.* 1910)

A CHARMING VIEW of the north side of the High Street, as it used to look in c. 1910, with its row of predominantly weatherboarded cottages – most of them with varying roof heights. Outside one-legged John Dann's barber's shop stands a hand-car used to deliver small packages sent by rail. Several of these cottages have since been demolished, including the barber's and, further along, the two-storeyed property behind the gas lamp where the War Memorial was erected in 1920.

MAYFIELD ERECTED ITS WAR MEMORIAL in front of the church of St Dunstan, in the space made by the demolition of a two-storeyed house which had once been Miss Emma Bridger's private school. The memorial was unveiled by General Schlater on 26 November 1920 and the Guard of Honour was formed by twenty-six men of the Royal Engineers who were then serving at Maresfield Camp.

THE SIXTH COMPANY OF THE ROYAL SUSSEX REGIMENT assemble along Mayfield High Street in c.1916. The house behind them was demolished in 1937 and many of its old frames and timbers were used in the extensive refurbishment of the neighbouring restaurant. The position of the barber's pole marked James Taylor's combined business of hairdresser and tobacconist. This is now the position of Mayfield's famous village sign, which won a £500 second prize in a national competition organized by the *Daily Mail* in 1920

MEMBERS OF THE LOCAL FIRE BRIGADE pose proudly on their Dennis fire engine outside the convent gateway in *c.* 1935. The crew members were originally unpaid volunteers and here include Charlie Jenner, Leo Unstead, Jack Smith, Bert Morris, Joe Wicker and Percy Skinner. The Fire Station originally stood behind the Royal Oak, before moving to Fletching Street and, more recently, to its current site. In the early days the crew was called out by telephoning fishmonger Percy Skinner (Tel. No. Mayfield 1) who would then run around the village – often helped by local boys like Eddie Eaton – knocking on each door.

MAYFIELD CONVENT was established as a boarding school for girls after the ruins of the old Palace (originally erected for the Archbishops of Canterbury in the tenth century) were presented to the Sisters of the Order of the Holy Child Jesus in 1863. Some of the renovation was carried out by the eminent Victorian architect E.W. Pugin. Written in French on this early 1901 picture postcard is the information that the elegantly uniformed girls are being supervised in their studies by Miss Livick.

MEMBERS OF THE MAYFIELD BRANCH OF THE BRITISH LEGION proudly march around Convent Corner after the wreath-laying ceremony at the War Memorial to commemorate their fallen comrades of the First World War. At the front of the procession are Captain Harris and Mr Searle while behind march: Jim Bale, Jim Taylor, Harry and Ern Carpenter, Will Pope, Evelyn Fenner, Tom Tremaine, Ted Coles, Henry Hall, Fred Foard, Archie Napper, Jim Saunders and hundreds of ex-servicemen. (*c.* 1922)

MAYFIELD'S NATIONAL SCHOOL was built on the Fletching Street junction at Convent Corner in 1814, paid for partly by local subscription and partly from a National Society grant. It was a mixed school until a new block was added for the girls in 1851 and a further room for infants in 1873. This *c.* 1905 postcard shows an entrance porch on the left. Among the more obvious additions, a gable end and the Round Room have been built on to the original building.

THERE ARE NOT MANY SMILES to be seen on the faces of the boys in this Mayfield School photograph taken in July 1895. Are they merely concentrating because of the long exposure time required for the plate photograph or has their natural joviality been suppressed by the grim faced schoolmaster, Mr John Bunsuall (headmaster 1886–1900) in the doorway? Top row: A Powell, A. Hatfield, A. Pollard, A. Manser, E. Miles, W. Pankhurst, J. Akehurst. Middle row: R. Pettit, E. Pelling, E. Saunders, A. Fenner, T. Wickens, J. Bale, R. Richardson, P. Jenner, C. Medhurst, R. Howell, C. Pennigar. Front row: L. Wicker, A. Heasman, G. Rogers, H. Saunders, J. Stonytrut, G. Lustead, T. Foard, W. Pearson, J. Hartfield, R. Wicker.

THE ROUND ROOM (designed by Mr Romaine Walker) under construction in 1913. To the left can be seen the gable end of the girls school and, to the right, the distinctive bell tower. Teddy Crowley of South Street has his bricklayers, masons and carpenters pose for a team photograph on their larch pole scaffolding, tied and tightened with scaffold cords. The uprights stand firmly in barrels filled with sand.

LOOKING ALONG FLETCHING STREET, with the entrance to the school on the left. The distinctive bell tower used to sit astride the old boys school. Further down the hill can be seen Charity Cottages. Local tradition maintains this tall building was the haunt of smugglers. Because of the steep fall of the ground, a secret second cellar was built below the first one, allowing a perfect hiding place for smuggled goods. (*c.* 1914)

EVEN THE PROXIMITY OF THE CARPENTER'S ARMS on the left cannot lure the pedestrian with his straw boater as he ambles down Fletching Street. Adjoining the cottage behind the gas lamp there used to be a small sweet shop. (1916)

LOOKING UP POUND HILL, the steep part of Fletching Street, before David Pratt turned the shop into a butcher's in c. 1910 and passed on his name to the junction, now called Pratt's Corner. In this c. 1908 postcard the shop is run by L. Honisett, who describes himself as a 'Grocer, Provision Merchant and General Draper'. The lane behind the ornate gas lamp is The Avenue, linking Fletching Street to Back Lane (now South Street).

THE AVENUE leads from Pratt's Corner to South Street. The lane is a cutting formed to offer an alternative route to avoid the steep hill on Fletching Street, which was only passable in the winter by ox-drawn waggons. (*c.* 1938)

HOOPERS FARM is sited south of Mayfield, down the steep Bat Hill which leads off Vale Road. In farmer Ephraim Eaton's day it used to be a large mixed farm, with its dairy to the right of the main farmhouse (which has been much altered over the years). The twitten leading off on the right has the charming name of Dawlin's Folly. (1909)

JAMES SAMUEL PAINE'S BLACKSMITH'S SHOP stood alongside the Rose and Crown (the building set back on the right) at Fletching Street. After The First World War James Downer operated a small car repair workshop on the premises and had a petrol pump outside.

THE JUNCTION OF FLETCHING STREET AND COGGIN'S MILL LANE sweeps past Jim Paine's smithy – with his Model T Ford parked on the Green. Beyond the inn sign for the Rose and Crown, H. Targett set up his bakehouse and confectionery business, calling it The Warren Bakery after the area.

THE BUILDINGS OPPOSITE THE ROSE AND CROWN mostly date back only to the turn of the century, with the exception of the then weatherboarded gable-end of the cottages of The Warren (now exposed as half-timbered). The single-storey shop behind the horse-drawn cart served as a greengrocer's, while at its rear Mr Manser had a bootmaker's workshop. (1908)

A BAKER'S BOY trudges along East Street – originally called Luggers Crouch – carrying his wicker delivery basket. At the time of this *c.* 1905 photograph the shop on the right was Jim Paine's grocery and ironmonger's business. By 1910 it had become Cecil Ashwell's grocery store and also contained the sub-post office.

WARREN ROAD, now part of Alexandra Road, when it was still unmetalled. The houses were built in the mid-Victorian period (1860–70), with Welsh slate roofs, fancy tiling and bay windows with a sheltered porch running through. However, in order to keep costs down, some unseasoned local timber was also used in the construction.

ALEXANDRA TERRACE was built around the corner from the last illustration. Again the homes are in Victorian style, but this time each terrace is made up of four dwellings, there is a sharper pitch to the roof and there are rubbed arches above the doors and lower windows. The field at the end had for many years been a hop garden and then was made into allotments. In 1935 Dunstan's Croft was built in the field. The road has only been recently adopted. (*c*. 1910)

COGGINS MILL. There is much dispute about the site and the spelling of this mill (sometimes Caulkins; here captioned Colkins). The original site was probably over Penny bridge where a flat field possibly marks where the mill pond stood. A motorbike and side-car stands outside Bill Balcombe's shop where he ran a general grocery store, an off-licence and the sub-post office. He used the thatched cottage alongside (now demolished) as a store for paraffin and tallow candles.

HOPS BEING PICKED from the pulled poles and put into the bin (a hessian bag supported on a wooden frame) at James Baker's Luckhurst Crouch Farm. Many farms throughout the area had their own small hop gardens, and used local labour for the hop picking. Left to right: Eddie Eaton, Charity Ann Skinner, John Hammond, Ethel Eaton, Boaz Eaton. On the far right, carrying the hop-laden pole, is farmer James Baker. (1924)

ARGOS HILL WINDMILL, a post-mill on a single-storey tarred roundhouse, stands on top of the 605-ft high Argos Hill to the north of Mayfield. A mill has stood on this site for centuries but this post-mill dates from 1835 when Aaron (?) Weston had it constructed. Aaron Weston also operated Merrieweathers watermill while his brother Edward worked Luggers Crouch windmill. It continued to operate until 1927 and remains in fine condition, still containing its original machinery. The Sussex Tailpole fan-tackle at the rear, operated on a pair of small wheels, swivels the main structure to allow the mill-sweeps to face the wind.

LOOKING NORTH ALONG THE MAIN MARK CROSS ROAD towards Argos Hill which was dominated by the post-mill before all the modern houses masked it. The small community around the hill used to have its own alehouse (The Chequers ?), a blacksmith's forge and a small general store. Apparently there are so many telephone lines on the poles because continental telephone links were originally routed through Mayfield.

A GENTLEMAN IN A POORLY FITTING JACKET poses awkwardly outside the Bicycle Arms at Argos Hill. He is presumably the assistant of the Heathfield photographer, A.D. Hellier, and has been planted there to add some animation to an otherwise empty street scene. (*c.* 1930)

MAYFIELD STRICT BAPTIST SUNDAY SCHOOL in *c.* 1902. Most of the children of the village must be here – and all in their Sunday best. What a beautiful array of bonnets, in particular. It was then still traditional for girls to have their heads covered at church. The photographer was Elam Whapham who was later to be clerk to the Parish Council.

AT PENNYBRIDGE, almost two miles north of Mayfield on what used to be the main road to Tunbridge Wells, a Roman Catholic residential school for boys was founded in 1868, run by the Xaverian Brothers. The building used to be an orphanage and was set in beautiful grounds with its own adjoining farm. An unlikely element of this religious institution is that the pupils were encouraged to take part in military training in the college's army cadet corps. I doubt if their training prepared them adequately for the horrors of trench warfare in the approaching First World War though. (*c.* 1910)

A CLASS OF PUPILS at the Xaverian College, Mayfield. No need for a governmentally imposed National Curriculum to enforce educational standards on these students as they sit in rows, underneath the gas lamps, apparently concentrating hard on the books lying open on their desks. I bet they weren't so well behaved when neither the teacher – nor the photographer – were present. (*c.* 1910)

THE MAYFIELD BAND. Many of the villages in this area of the Sussex Weald have a tradition of uniformed silver or brass bands: for instance, Mayfield is known to have had a brass band as early as 1885. It is interesting to see the number of stringed instruments present in this photograph taken in the grounds of the Old Vicarage in *c.* 1920.

TWO CRICKET TEAMS, smartly turned out in their whites, club blazers and hats, pose for the photographer on the steps of the old pavilion at Cogger's field in *c.* 1900. Mayfield Cricket Club has now completed a distinguished century of play.

ACKNOWLEDGEMENTS

R. & K. Lower • Joe Cornford • Jack Cornford • F. Feist • E. & J. Phillips
S.C. Phillips • C.E. Phillips • Mrs E. Tachauer • R. & M. Lambert-Gorwyn
P. Love • Miss B. Gardner • A. Dallaway • T. Dallaway • Mrs M. Watson
P. Burgess • P. Cole • Mrs M. Keeley • Henry Crouch • E. Eaton
Crown Hotel • B. Delves • S. Baldwin • B.G. Russell • R. & D. Piper
Tim Watson • Mrs Watson • E. Vine • A.W. Bousell • D. Hook • R. Ticehurst
B. Delves • G. Baker